ALONE IN MAJESTY

WILLIAM MACDONALD

OLIVER
NELSON

THOMAS NELSON PUBLISHERS
Nashville

Published in Nashville, Tennessee, by Oliver-Nelson Books, a division of Thomas Nelson, Inc., Publishers, and distributed in Canada by Word Communications, Ltd., Richmond, British Columbia.

The Bible version used in this publication is THE NEW KING JAMES VERSION. Copyright © 1979, 1980, 1982, Thomas Nelson, Inc., Publishers. Scripture quotations noted NASB are from the New American Standard Bible, © 1960, 1962, 1963, 1968, 1971, 1972, 1973, 1975, 1977 by The Lockman Foundation. Used by permission. Scripture quotations noted PHILLIPS are from J. B. Phillips: THE NEW TESTAMENT IN MODERN ENGLISH, Revised Edition. © J. B. Phillips 1958, 1960, 1972. Used by permission of Macmillan Publishing Co., Inc. Scripture quotations noted KJV are from the King James Version of the Holy Bible.

Every effort has been made to contact the owners or owners' agents of copyrighted material for permission to use their material. If copyrighted material has been included without the correct copyright notice or without permission, due to error or failure to locate owners/agents or otherwise, we apologize for the error or omission and ask that the owner or owner's agent contact Oliver-Nelson and supply appropriate information. Correct information will be included in any reprinting.

Library of Congress Cataloging-in-Publication Data

MacDonald, William, 1917–
    Alone in majesty / William MacDonald.
      p. cm.
    Includes bibliographical references.
    ISBN 0-8407-9247-6
    1. God—Attributes. I. Title.
BT130.M33 1994
231'.4—dc20   93-36662
                                                CIP

Printed in the United States of America

1 2 3 4 5 6 — 99 98 97 96 95 94

Contents

My God, how wonderful Thou art,
Thy majesty how bright,
How beautiful Thy mercy seat,
In depths of burning light!

How wonderful, how beautiful
The sight of Thee must be
Thine endless wisdom, boundless
  pow'r,
And awesome purity!
                    —Frederick William Faber

For this is God,
Our God forever and ever;
He will be our guide
Even to death.

                    —Psalm 48:14

Introduction

The existence of God is the foundation of all religion.

—Stephen Charnock

The fact of the existence of God means that we as human beings are accountable. If there is a Supreme Creator and Sustainer, the creatures are responsible to Him. American statesman Daniel Webster said that the most profound thought he ever had was his accountability to God.

If evolution were true, there would be no moral standards for society. If we were the product of blind chance, of a random assembling of molecules, no one could find fault with wars, murders, thefts, or any antisocial behavior. People would not be responsible to any higher authority.

The apostle Paul points out in Romans 1 that

everyone knows that there is a God. His existence is revealed in creation; creation demands a Creator, and design demands a Designer. And it is revealed in conscience; we all have an innate consciousness of right and wrong. The works that the law requires are written in our hearts.

The heathen do not *want* to retain the true God in their knowledge. They know that belief in such a God would cramp their life-styles. So they turn to idolatry. They make images of people, birds, animals, and snakes and then worship them. Since each successive image represents a downward step in the scale of creation, it follows that they feel less and less responsible to live clean lives. If their god is a snake, it doesn't really matter how they live. This explains the close link between idolatry and immorality. Idols made by human beings do not make moral demands on their worshipers.

We all become like what we worship. Whether we worship money, sinful humanity, carnal pleasures, material possessions, or carved images, we begin to resemble them. On the other hand, the more we worship God, the more we grow into His image (2 Cor. 3:18).

Belief determines behavior. That is why it is so important to have true views of God. The higher our thoughts of Him, the more our lives will be exalted, holy, and glorious.

Some of God's attributes are unique to Him.

They are *incommunicable*, that is, they cannot be shared by us. For instance, only God is omnipotent, omniscient, and omnipresent. We will never be immutable or infinite. Although believers will live forever, they are not eternal because they do have a beginning. In Part One, we will be discussing these unique or incommunicable attributes.

But God also shares some of His attributes with humanity. These are called *communicable* attributes. We will discuss them in Part Two. Of course, we can never have these qualities in their perfect forms. Ours will always be weak, pale reflections of His. But we can love, be holy, and show mercy. We can be just and truthful, show grace and goodness. And because we can, we should. That is how we become imitators of God (Eph. 5:1).

The purpose of our study then is not merely to know about God's attributes but to cultivate the shared or communicable ones in our daily Christian life.

Now we must move on to a study of the attributes of God. It is usually by reciting His attributes that we define God. For instance, the Shorter Catechism says, "God is a Spirit, infinite, eternal, and unchangeable in His being, wisdom, power, holiness, justice, goodness, and truth."

A serious study of God's characteristics will

inevitably lead us to worship Him more sincerely, to trust Him more wholly, to serve Him more faithfully, and to seek to be more conformed to Him in all our ways.

Part One

Unique
Attributes
of God

Who is like You, O Lord, among the
* gods?*
Who is like You, glorious in holiness,
Fearful in praises, doing wonders?

> —From the Song of Moses
> (Exod. 15:11)

— 1 —

One True God

Hear, O Israel: The LORD our God, the LORD is one!

—Deuteronomy 6:4

The Bible teaches that there is one and only one true God. He is the God who revealed Himself to Abraham and his descendants. But He was also known from the dawn of time by those who withstood polytheism and idolatry.

The modern view is that people believed in many gods and only gradually, due to the brilliance of Hebrew prophets, came to believe in monotheism. The Bible teaches quite the opposite: from the very beginning God revealed that He is one—and the one and only true God.

The verse at the head of this chapter is the creed of Judaism, the *Shema* (pronounced sh'MAH); it means "hear" in Hebrew and is the first word of the creed.

3

When we say that God is one, we mean that He is a pure spirit being, not composed of parts as we are (spirit, soul, and body).[1] In saying that God is one, however, it should be pointed out that Hebrew has two words for oneness, one suggesting absolute numerical oneness, and the other suggesting a unity somewhat like our word *united*. The second of these words is used for God.[2]

Old Testament verses that stress the uniqueness and the unity of God include the following words from King Solomon's benediction at the dedication of the temple: "That all the peoples of the earth may know that the LORD is God; there is no other" (1 Kings 8:60). And one of the minor prophets predicts,

> And the LORD shall be King
>   over all the earth.
> In that day it shall be—
> "The LORD is one,"
> And His name one (Zech. 14:9).

God is unique. He is one—the only one. No one else should share His glory, not even an archangel, the Virgin Mary, or any saint, prophet, or apostle.

The New Testament continues the absolute monotheism of the Old Testament, as the following verses indicate.

Mark 12:29–30 shows that Christ considered

the *Shema* as the foundation of true religion, as did His Jewish compatriots: "Jesus answered him, 'The first of all the commandments is: "Hear, O Israel, the LORD our God, the LORD is one. And you shall love the LORD your God with all your heart, with all your soul, with all your mind, and with all your strength."'"

In John 17:3, in our Lord's great high-priestly prayer, He mentions the unity and uniqueness of the one true God in connection with the fact that He sent His Son, and that eternal life consists in knowing God through Christ. This is done by faith, as the rest of the Bible teaches. (See, for example, Gen. 15:6 and Eph. 2:8–9.)

Regarding the multitude of false gods in the world, the apostle Paul writes,

> Therefore concerning the eating of things offered to idols, we know that an idol is nothing in the world, and that there is no other God but one. For even if there are so-called gods, whether in heaven or on earth (as there are many gods and many lords), yet for us there is one God, the Father, of whom are all things, and we for Him; and one Lord Jesus Christ, through whom are all things, and through whom we live (1 Cor. 8:4–6).

While it is true that there is only one God, now that the Savior has come to earth, we need to know God the Son in order to reach the Father: "For there is one God and one Mediator between God and men, the Man Christ Jesus" (1 Tim. 2:5). This verse also cuts out go-be-tweens such as Michael the Archangel, Joseph, the Virgin Mary, or any other of the saints.

Organized religions such as Judaism, Christendom, and Islam[3] teach monotheism, that there is only one God. This is good, but it is not enough. James tells us this clearly: "You believe that there is one God. You do well. Even the demons believe—and tremble!" (2:19).

The genuine relationship we should have with the one true God is expressed in these lines inspired by the ancient Hebrew *Shema:*

> The Lord our God is one Lord;
>   Not many gods have we;
> Unique and indivisible,
>   Alone in majesty.
>
> Him we should love with all our heart,
>   With all our souls adore,
> Give Him the best of mind and strength
>   And praise Him evermore!

Notes

1. Of course, in the Incarnation, God the Son took on a human body through the miracle of the virgin birth. For all eternity there will be a God-man on the throne—with a glorified, spiritual body.

2. The Hebrew words are *echād* and *yāchîd,* respectively. The choice of words in the *Shema* allows for the doctrine of the Trinity (see next chapter). The word *echād* indicates a compound unity, as of a bunch of grapes—several grapes making up one cluster. The other word (*yāchîd)* is used for an only child in Jeremiah 6:26.

3. The God of the Hebrews in the Old Testament is the same as the God and Father of our Lord Jesus Christ. Allah, the deity as taught by Mohammed, is of a very different nature indeed.

— 2 —

Three Persons in One

Go therefore and make disciples of all the nations, baptizing them in the name of the Father and of the Son and of the Holy Spirit, teaching them to observe all things that I have commanded you; and lo, I am with you always, even to the end of the age.

—Matthew 28:19–20

The above parting words of our Lord Jesus Christ show that the baptismal formula that officially marks out a believer as a Christian and identifies the person with the church, which is the body of Christ, is trinitarian. This means the

8

formula recognizes that God is a Trinity or, more precisely, a triunity.

But what does it mean to say that our God is triune or a Trinity?

One thing is certain: it does not mean that Christians worship three gods (tritheism)! Some antitrinitarians have made this charge. As we have seen, our God is one. But He is also three. How can God be one and three at the same time? The answer is that He is one in a different way from the way He is three. As to His essence, God is definitely one. There is only one God. Yet this one God subsists or exists in three persons; there are three *distinct* entities in the Godhead.

Also, it does not mean that God is one but merely manifests Himself in three different modes or ways at different times. Some false teachers have said that the Father is the Son and the Son is the Holy Spirit. This heresy is called *modalism*, from the notion that the one God merely appears in history under three different modes.

Some people who oppose the Trinity (and nearly all false cults do so) point out that the word *Trinity* does not occur in the Bible. Granted. Neither do many other useful theological terms that summarize biblical teachings (Millennium, virgin birth, eternal security, for example). The important thing is that the truth about the Trinity is taught in God's Word. Our word *Trinity* is merely the English form of the Latin term *trinitas*, coined in the third century. A word such as *triunity* (three in one) would have been even more precise, but it is too late to alter a seventeen-hundred-year-old term.

The Old Testament, as we have seen, stresses the unity of God. Even there, however, the Hebrew word for one that is used for God means not an absolute numerical, solitary oneness but something like united. The reason God stressed His unity to His Old Testament people, I believe, is that the Israelites were surrounded on every hand by polytheistic Gentile idolaters. Before they could learn the truth of God's threeness, they had to be well-grounded in His oneness and His spirituality. Only after the Babylonian captivity was Israel cured of going after the many heathen gods.

The very first verse in the Bible, "In the beginning God created the heavens and the earth" (Gen. 1:1), gives at least a hint, in the Hebrew original, of the triunity of God. The Hebrew word for God here is *Elohim*, a masculine plural noun that in pagan contexts is translated "gods." Yet the verb translated "create" (*bārā'*) is a masculine singular verb. It is not normal to have a plural noun with a singular verb. (It would be like "The men is" in English.) Many scholars counter that *Elohim* is simply a plural of *majesty*. This is grammatically possible. Later in Genesis, however, God speaks of Himself as "We" and "Us" and "Our image" (1:26; 3:22; 11:7). Here the real plurality of persons united as one God is strongly implied.[1] At any rate, this is the revelation that will gradually unfold as the Bible progresses till we reach the New Testament, where the three persons in the Godhead are clearly revealed.

Another Old Testament revelation of the nature of God that conforms to the teaching of the Trinity concerns the appearances of the Angel (or Messenger) of the Lord (Jehovah or Yahweh). He appears in human form to people and yet is recognized as God. For example, Hagar sees Him and identifies Him as the God who sees her (Gen. 16:7–14). To Moses, in the very crucial burning bush passage (Exod. 3:2–6), the same Angel of the Lord appears as God. Yet later, God speaks and refers to sending "My Angel" before His people (Exod. 33:2–3). Also, Hosea writes of Jacob that "he struggled with *God*. Yes, he struggled with the *Angel*" (Hos. 12:3–4, emphasis added).

How can the Angel of the Lord be God and His Messenger at the same time? If God were an absolutely numerically unitarian being, it would be impossible. But this revelation is explained by the doctrine of the Trinity. The Angel of the

Lord is indeed God—God the Son in His preincarnate state. He is distinct from God the Father
who sends Him. They are separate persons, yet
with the Holy Spirit, they constitute the one true
God.

There are other inklings of the Trinity in the
Old Testament as well. In the Aaronic benedic-
tion of Numbers 6:24–26, the name "the Lord"
(Jehovah or Yahweh) is repeated three times. In
Isaiah 6:3, the seraphim cry to one another, say-
ing,

> Holy, holy, holy
>   is the Lord of hosts;
> The whole earth is
>   full of His glory!

These famous texts do not prove the Trinity,
but they certainly comport with that truth very
well.

A remarkable Old Testament verse that de-
serves to be better known by trinitarians includes the "Lord God" (the Father), "His
Spirit," and the One who was "sent" ("Me," that
is, the Son):

> Come near to Me, hear this:
> I have not spoken in secret from the beginning;
> From the time that it was, I was there.
> And now the *Lord God* and *His Spirit*
> Have sent *Me* (Isa. 48:16, emphasis added).

As the footnote in the New King James Version indicates, a singular verb is used in Hebrew for "have," which indicates the oneness of the persons.[2]

In the New Testament, the revelation of the holy Trinity becomes quite clear.

At our Lord's baptism, all three divine persons were present:

> It came to pass in those days that Jesus came from Nazareth of Galilee, and was baptized by John in the Jordan. And immediately, coming up from the water, He saw the heavens parting and the Spirit descending upon Him like a dove. Then a voice came from heaven, "You are My beloved Son, in whom I am well pleased" (Mark 1:9–11).

The Son standing in the Jordan, the Father's presence manifesting itself by the voice from heaven, and the Spirit showing Himself as a dove coming down upon the Son of God give us a picture of the Trinity in action.

In Galatians 4:4–6, we see all three persons of the Trinity working together for our salvation:

> But when the fullness of the time had come, *God* sent forth *His Son*, born of a woman, born under the law, to redeem those who were under the law, that we might receive the adoption as sons. And because you are sons, God has sent forth

the *Spirit* of His Son into your hearts, crying out,
"Abba, Father!" (emphasis added).

Other passages showing all three persons together include 1 Corinthians 12:3–6; Ephesians
4:4–6; and 1 Peter 1:2.

In His famous and beautiful Upper Room
Discourse, our Lord reveals some of the rela-
tionships between the persons of the Trinity.
Two verses that are similar, yet slightly different,
are John 14:26 and 15:26:

> But the Helper, the *Holy Spirit*, whom the *Father*
> will send in My name, He will teach you all
> things, and bring to your remembrance all things
> that *I* said to you (emphasis added).

> But when the Helper comes, whom I shall send
> to you from the *Father*, the *Spirit of truth* who
> proceeds from the Father, He will testify of *Me*
> (emphasis added).

Since the doctrine of the Trinity is difficult to
understand, some Bible scholars have used illustrations of a threefold character from nature. Actually, the very difficulty of the doctrine shows
that it is not a humanly devised teaching but a
divine revelation that must be received by faith.
No mere humanly conceived religion would ever
have come up with what seems so illogical.[3]

A well-known example of trying to teach the

Trinity through nature is Patrick's use of the shamrock to illustrate the three-in-one character of God. It was a charming illustration for his time perhaps, but it will hardly do today.

Other natural analogies are built on space, matter, and time. Space is generally seen as threefold in its measurement: height, width, and depth. Matter is also threefold: it can be a liquid, solid, or gas. Water is the best illustration of this: liquid (water), solid (ice), or gas (steam). Time is divided into past, present, and future, and yet all are time.

These triads in nature do witness indirectly to the expression of the deity in threeness, but their weakness is that they all lack personality.

A person, comprised of spirit, soul, and body (1 Thess. 5:23), is a better analogy. A human being is one entity made up of three parts. When God made us in His own image, the threefold nature was probably at least part of the meaning of how we are like God.

Augustine, in his scholarly exposition on the Trinity (*De Trinitate*), used two analogies that are superior to natural illustrations. He was not completely satisfied with them, but they have been a help to many thoughtful Christians, so let us look at them briefly.

One of the analogies is that the Trinity is like Speaker, Spoken, and Speaking. The Father, who is presented as the sender, source, and initiator in the Godhead, is the Speaker. The Son is Spoken. This fits in with John 1:1 where Christ is the Word, the expression of God's thoughts to the world. The Spirit, the active agent of the Trinity on earth, especially now that Christ has ascended, is Speaking. Through the Word that He inspired and through His Spirit-filled human agents, He is still speaking to today's world. And yet, they are all essentially one, Speaker, Spoken, and Speaking.

A second analogy is more popular and is based on the truth that "God is love" (1 John 4:8). Augustine, a brilliant thinker, wondered how God in eternity past could be love when He had no object to love. Love must have an object, and perfect love even demands love for a mutually loved object. For example, a husband and a wife can love each other very deeply and be happy in their love. But when a child, the fruit of their mutual love, comes along, their shared love for this extension of their love is perfected. In the New Testament, the Father is emphasized as the One who loved (the Lover); the Son is the Loved ("My beloved Son"); the active creative bond between them is seen as the Spirit (Love).

The doctrine of the blessed Trinity is a uniquely Christian teaching. Modern Judaism, Islam, and "liberal" Christendom, not to mention the cults—both ancient and modern—reject this great truth. Any group that denies the doctrine of the Trinity is outside the fold of true Christianity. Since the early days of the church, the trinitarian understanding of God has been the hallmark of the faith.

The Trinity is not merely theology, it is how God has revealed Himself—how He really is— "God in three persons, blessed Trinity." A unitarian god would never satisfy the tripartite being of humankind. We are made in God's image. Part of that image, as we have seen, is trinitarian.

The English poet-preacher George Herbert expressed these truths exquisitely in these poetic lines:

> The whole world round
> Is not enough to fill the heart's three corners;
> But yet it craveth still;
> Only the Trinity that made it can
> Suffice the vast triangled heart of man!

I close with another clear reference to the Trinity in the New Testament from the pen of the apostle Paul: "The grace of the Lord Jesus Christ, and the love of God, and the communion of the Holy Spirit be with you all. Amen" (2 Cor. 13:14).

Notes

1. It should be noted that Genesis 1:2 mentions the Spirit of God, whom we later learn is the Holy Spirit, the third person of the Trinity.

2. English grammatical usage demands a plural verb here.

3. The claim that Hinduism also has a trinity is not valid. The three, a sort of triad in Hindu lore, are not three in one. In fact "the destroyer" and "the creator" are quite at odds in that teaching. The triad merely constitutes three more gods out of the literally thousands in that ancient religion.

— 3 —

The Uncreated Source of Life

For as the Father has life in Himself, so He has granted the Son to have life in Himself.

—John 5:26

As the words of our Lord Jesus quoted above show, the triune Godhead is the fountain of all life.

The eternity of God is linked with His self-existence. He does not owe His existence to anyone or anything outside Himself. His life was uncreated. It was not something that was given to Him. The source of His being is entirely in Himself.

This quality of self-existence is implied in the

19

very name of God: "I AM WHO I AM" (Exod. 3:14).[1] Although the name has many meanings, it includes the truth that God's being had no cause outside Himself.

Contemplation of the self-existence of God should evoke praise and worship. What a great God He is! How indescribable are His excellencies! How matchless is His person!

At the same time, we should be grateful to the Fountain of life that He has chosen to give life to us. Life is a gift of God. Every breath we take is a merciful gift from Him: "He gives to all life, breath, and all things . . . for in Him we live and move and have our being" (Acts 17:25, 28). Let us always be thankful for natural life and, even more, for the gift of eternal life through Jesus Christ, our Lord.

A still popular medieval hymn[2] speaks of the second person of the Godhead as the fountain or source of all life or existence:

> Jesus, Thou joy of loving hearts,
> Thou Fount of Life, Thou Light of men,
> From the best bliss that earth imparts,
> We turn unfilled to Thee again.

Notes

1. The covenant name of God, Jehovah (or Yahweh), is probably derived from the Hebrew verb

hāyāh (to be). It is translated "LORD" in many major Bible versions.

2. The hymn dates from about 1150 and is called *Jesu dulcis memoria* in the original Latin. It is often attributed to Bernard of Clairvaux (1090–1153). This translation was done by Ray Palmer (1808–87).

— 4 —

The Self-Sufficient Lord

Nor is He worshiped with men's hands, as though He needed anything, since He gives to all life, breath, and all things.

—Acts 17:25

Our Lord is completely self-sufficient. He does not depend on anyone or anything outside Himself for His happiness. He needs nothing from His creatures.

In Psalm 50:10–12, we hear Him saying,

> For every beast of the forest is Mine,
> And the cattle on a thousand hills.
> I know all the birds of the mountains,
> And the wild beasts of the field are Mine.

If I were hungry, I would not tell you;
For the world is Mine, and all its fullness.

David acknowledged the self-sufficiency of God: "All things come from You, and of Your own we have given You" (1 Chron. 29:14).

J. I. Packer writes,

God was happy without man before man was made; He would have continued happy had He simply destroyed man after man had sinned; but as it is He has set His love upon particular sinners, and this means that, by His own free voluntary choice, He will not know perfect and unmixed happiness again till He has brought every one of them to heaven. He has in effect resolved that henceforth for all eternity His happiness shall be conditional upon ours. Thus God saves, not only for His glory, but also for His gladness. This goes far to explain why it is that there is joy (God's own joy) in the presence of the angels when a sinner repents (Luke 15:10), and why there will be "exceeding joy" when God sets us faultless at the last day in His own holy presence (Jude 24). The thought passes understanding and almost beggars belief, but there is no doubt that, according to Scripture, such is the love of God.[1]

The self-sufficiency of God is a doctrine that greatly glorifies Him. God is splendid and majestic in His independence. He contains all that

He needs, and He does not receive anything that He has not already given. A. W. Tozer expressed it well:

> Were all human beings suddenly to become blind, still the sun would shine by day and the stars by night, for these owe nothing to the millions who benefit by their light. So, were every man on earth to become atheist, it could not affect God in any way. He is what He is in Himself without regard to any other. To believe in Him adds nothing to His perfections; to doubt Him takes nothing away.[2]

This doctrine reduces us to our proper size. It strikes a deathblow to human pride. God doesn't need us. He doesn't need our help. He doesn't need us to defend Him. He doesn't need our service. When we give Him anything, we give Him only what is His own. Although God does seek our worship, He can exist without it, and He did so for ages. To hear people talk today, you'd think that God was fortunate when some prominent, talented person becomes a believer. That is arrogant nonsense! All the benefit is on our side, not on God's.

And yet He does seek our fellowship. As Jesus said to the woman of Samaria, "The hour is coming, and now is, when the true worshipers will worship the Father in spirit and truth; for the Father is seeking such to worship Him" (John 4:23).

And although we continue to insist that God doesn't need His creatures, a poet, whose initials are T. P., can speak of a divine need and get away with it:

> Can it be that in the glory
> Ere of Him I had a thought,
> He was yearning o'er the lost one,
> Whom His precious blood had bought?
> That it was *His* need that brought Him
> Down to the accursed tree?
> Deeper than His deep compassion
> Wondrous thought! *His* need of me.

Annie Johnson Flint continues the paradox of the self-existent One by reminding us that

> Christ has no hands but our hands
> To do His work today;
> He has no feet but our feet
> To lead men in His way;
> He has no lips but our lips
> To tell men how He died;
> He has no help but our help
> To bring them to His side.[3]

All this is poetic license, of course. The fact remains that God is self-sufficient, that He needs no one and nothing outside Himself.

We rejoice in the self-sufficiency of God. We accept the truth as absolutely imperative if God is to be God. We stand in awe and admiration of His solitary independence. We worship and adore. Johann Scheffler noted this wondrous attribute:

> Fountain of good, all blessing flows
> From Thee; no want Thy fullness knows;
> What but Thyself canst Thou desire?
> Yet, self-sufficient as Thou art,
> Thou dost desire my worthless heart;
> This, only this, dost Thou require.

Notes

1. J. I. Packer, *Knowing God,* p. 138.
2. A. W. Tozer, *The Knowledge of the Holy,* p. 40.
3. Used by permission of Scripture Press.

— 5 —

Knowledge Without Limit

God . . . knows all things.

—1 John 3:20

God is omniscient; He has perfect knowledge of everything. There is nothing that He does not know. He has never learned and never can. It is not enough to say that He could know everything if He wanted to. He does know everything! He has always been omniscient and always will be. A. W. Tozer elaborates for us:

God knows instantly and effortlessly all matter and all matters, all mind and every mind, all spirit and all spirits, all being and every being, all creaturehood and all creatures, every plurality and all pluralities, all law and every law, all relations, all causes, all thoughts, all mysteries, all

enigmas, all feeling, all desires, every unuttered
secret, all thrones and dominions, all personali-
ties, all things visible and invisible in heaven and
in earth, motion, space, time, life, death, good,
evil, heaven, and hell.[1]

One of the key passages on the omniscience of
God is Psalm 139:1–6:

> O LORD, You have searched me and known me.
> You know my sitting down and my rising up;
> You understand my thought afar off.
> You comprehend my path and my lying down,
> And are acquainted with all my ways.
> For there is not a word on my tongue,
> But behold, O LORD, You know it altogether.
> You have hedged me behind and before,
> And laid Your hand upon me.
> Such knowledge is too wonderful for me;
> It is high, I cannot attain it.

When the psalmist considers the infinite
knowledge of the Lord, he is struck with what
might be called sensory overload. He can't conceive of such knowledge; it is too amazing.

The Lord Jesus gave a comforting insight into
the omniscience of God when He pointed out
that not a sparrow falls to the ground without
our Father knowing (Matt. 10:29). Dr. Harry A.
Ironside put it vividly: "God attends the funeral
of every sparrow." Think of it! The God of

galaxies and supernovas is interested in a seemingly insignificant sparrow. And how much more does He care for His people! Mabel Brown Denison put this truth into verse:

> Of all of God's marvels transcendent,
> This wonder of wonders I see,
> That the God of such infinite greatness
> Should care for the sparrows—and me.

In Romans 11:33–36, Paul speaks with rhapsody of God's knowledge:

> Oh, the depth of the riches both of the wisdom and knowledge of God! How unsearchable are His judgments and His ways past finding out! "For who has known the mind of the LORD? Or who has become His counselor? Or who has first given to Him and it shall be repaid to him?" For of Him and through Him and to Him are all things, to whom be glory forever. Amen.

The writer of the book of Hebrews reminds us that "all things are naked and open to the eyes of Him to whom we must give account" (Heb. 4:13).

It is overpowering to think of all the knowledge of God. In our generation, we have witnessed an enormous knowledge explosion. In science, literature, philosophy, geography, history, and every other sphere, new books pour out in seemingly endless procession. Our libraries are glutted.

Specialization is the name of the game. Experts are proficient in only a small field; they can never hope to cover the spectrum. But God has full knowledge of everything in heaven and on earth, and He doles this knowledge out to people in thimblefuls. Whenever He does, these people are promptly acclaimed as discoverers.

But there is still so much we do *not* know. Though we can travel to the moon, we can't understand how a bee can fly. Though we can transplant human hearts, we can't cure the common cold. We can conquer outer space, but we cannot conquer inner space. We can make war, but we cannot make peace. We know so much, and yet we know so little. With God there are no mysteries, no insoluble problems, no puzzles.

And what is true of God the Father is also true of God the Son. Even as a man on earth, the second person of the Trinity was omniscient. When a woman touched the edge of His robe, He knew it was the touch of faith and not that of the thronging crowd (Luke 8:43–48). He knew exactly where the fish were in the Sea of Galilee (John 21:6). He knew what people were thinking (Matt. 9:4). He knew the character and history of those He met (John 1:47; 4:16–18). He was able to fortell the future, including His own betrayal, denial, crucifixion, resurrection, ascension, and coming again (John 13:11; Mark 14:30; Luke

9:22; John 14:2–3). The disciples were convinced that He knew everything (John 16:30).

It's true that some verses seem to say that His knowledge was limited. For instance, Luke says that "Jesus increased in wisdom and stature" (Luke 2:52). How can One who has perfect knowledge increase in wisdom? And Mark indicates that Jesus did not know the time of His second coming (Mark 13:32). How could this be if He was omniscient?

Here we come face-to-face with the mystery of the Incarnation: "Great is the mystery of godliness: God was manifested in the flesh" (1 Tim. 3:16). How deity and humanity can coexist in one person is beyond our understanding. Let me give an example. We know that God cannot die, and we know that Jesus is God. Yet Jesus died. How can that be? It is a mystery. There is a sense in which we cannot comprehend the person of Christ; only the Father can know Him (Matt. 11:27). Many of the most serious heresies have arisen as a result of theologians trying to solve the mystery. All they have succeeded in doing is detracting from His deity, His humanity, or both.

But we can know that, though He emptied Himself of His position in heaven to become a man, He never emptied Himself of the attributes of deity. He did not become God minus some of His attributes; that would be impossible. Rather,

He became God plus humanity. He did not lay aside the glory of deity; rather, He veiled that glory in a garb of flesh. If a prince leaves the royal palace to go and live in the slums, his position has changed, but he is still the same person. He can empty himself of his privileged place and veil his true identity, but he cannot empty himself of his personhood. So it was with the Lord Jesus. He did not consider His position with the Father in heaven something He had to hold on to at all costs. Instead, He came down to this planet as a man so that He might die for humankind. But He never ceased to have full knowledge of all things.

So if a couple of verses seem to indicate that His knowledge was limited, we acknowledge the difficulty but reject any explanation that denies His perfect omniscience at all times. We hold to the truth that "in Him dwells all the fullness of the Godhead bodily" (Col. 2:9), and that means He always possessed all the attributes of deity. He always had perfect knowledge of all things.

This attribute of God should have a profound effect on our lives. How we should honor the Lord as we muse on the infinite dimensions of His knowledge! How we should sing His praises!

The fact that God knows everything should deter sin. Since there is no such thing as secret sin, we should never try to fool ourselves into thinking that no one would know. As the saying goes, "Secret sin on earth is open scandal in heaven." God knows (Gen. 16:13). We can never sin and get away with it (Num. 32:23). At the same time, we should not think of Him as a frowning ogre, ready to pounce on us for each infraction. Rather, He is a loving heavenly Father whose commandments are designed for our welfare and happiness, not His own. Those who think of Him as hard to please and stern really don't know Him.

But it is also tremendously comforting to realize that God knows (Ps. 56:8). He knows what His people are going through—the sufferings, trials, persecutions, sorrows, and wrongs (Job 23:10): "In every pang that rends the heart, the Man of Sorrows has a part." The Lord Jesus wrote to the church in Smyrna, "I know your works, tribulation, and poverty" (Rev. 2:9). His "I know" conveys a world of sympathy and comfort.

What an encouragement it is to realize that God knew all about us, and yet He saved us anyway! He knew what failures and flops we would be, how we would wander away from Him and break His heart. And yet He threw His arms of love around us and justified us freely by His grace.

It's great to realize that God knows the worship and praise we feel in our hearts for Him but cannot find words to express. And He knows what we would like to do for Him but for one reason or another are prevented from doing. For instance, David wanted to build a temple for the Lord. The Lord said, in effect, "No, David, you can't build it—but never mind, it was good that it was in your heart." David will doubtless share in the reward for building the temple, even if Solomon had the actual privilege. In the same way, there are people who would like to go to the mission field but can't. There are generous Christians who would like to give more to the work of the Lord but don't have it to give. God knows all about it and will reward the desire.

Think of the greatness of God's knowledge—He can hear and understand prayer in so many different languages. We have heard of people who have mastered several languages. Robert Dick Wilson, a Christian Bible scholar, learned over forty rare and ancient tongues in order to better solve difficulties in the Old Testament text. But no one except God knows all languages.

In studying the attributes of God, we should seek to emulate many of them—His love, mercy, and grace, for instance. We will never come close to attaining His knowledge, but we should dedicate the very finest of our intellectual power to Him. We should ever be growing in the knowledge of God, in the knowledge of the Lord Jesus, and in the knowledge of the sacred Scriptures.

One final thought in connection with God's omniscience. When God forgives us, He forgets our sins. He buries them in the sea of His forgetfulness; He puts them behind His back—as far as the east is from the west. He'll never remember them again. Now how can an omniscient God forget? I don't know, but I know He does. Even if we admit that He forgets our sins in the sense that we will never be judged for them, the truth is as wonderful as ever.

How great God is! His greatness is unsearchable. He is greatly to be praised:

> For this is God,
> Our God forever and ever;
> He will be our guide
> Even to death (Ps. 48:14).

He has complete knowledge of everything, as this anonymous writer realized:

Though infinitely glorious and gloriously grand,
He knows the eternal story of every grain of sand.

Note

1. A. W. Tozer, *The Knowledge of the Holy,* p. 62.

— 6 —

The Almighty One

The Lord God Omnipotent reigns!

—Revelation 19:6

When we call God the Almighty, we call Him by His name because He has all might. He is all-powerful. There is nothing that He cannot do. He is the Lord God omnipotent.[1]

There is no question that the omnipotence of God is a favorite theme of the Bible writers. Consider the following, for example:

I am Almighty God; walk before Me and be blameless (Gen. 17:1).

Is anything too hard for the LORD? (Gen. 18:14).

I know that Thou canst do all things, and that

no purpose of Thine can be thwarted (Job 42:2 NASB).

> God has spoken once,
> Twice I have heard this:
> That power belongs to God (Ps. 62:11).

Ah, Lord GOD! Behold, You have made the heavens and the earth by Your great power and outstretched arm. There is nothing too hard for You (Jer. 32:17).

With God all things are possible (Matt. 19:26).

For with God nothing will be impossible (Luke 1:37).

Stephen Charnock wrote, "The power of God is that ability and strength whereby He can bring to pass whatsoever He please, whatsoever His infinite wisdom can direct, and whatsoever the infinite purity of His will can resolve."[2]

He is able to build us up and give us "an inheritance among all those who are sanctified" (Acts 20:32). He "is able to make all grace abound toward" us (2 Cor. 9:8). "He is able even to subdue all things to Himself" (Phil. 3:21). "He is able to aid those who are tempted" (Heb. 2:18). "He is also able to save to the uttermost those who come to God through Him" (Heb. 7:25). And He "is able to keep [us] from stumbling, and to present [us] faultless before the presence of His glory with exceeding joy" (Jude 24).

When we say that God can do anything, we obviously mean anything consistent with His moral virtues and His essential character. For example, God cannot lie (Num. 23:19; Heb. 6:18). "He cannot deny Himself" (2 Tim. 2:13). He "cannot be tempted by evil" (James 1:13). He cannot condone sin or look with favor on it (Hab. 1:13). Because He is timeless and immortal, He cannot age or die. He cannot swear by anyone greater than Himself (Heb. 6:13) simply because there is no one greater. But these limitations do not affect His omnipotence in the slightest. Neither do foolish questions such as, Can God make a stone too heavy for Himself to lift? Such questions are intellectual absurdities and not worthy of serious consideration.

The power of God is seen in the creation of the universe and the creation of humankind. He created the heavens and earth instantly, out of nothing, without tools, by a word. Think of the power that spangled the heavens with stars, planets, and galaxies that are spread out in space for billions of light-years. Consider the power that creates the human body in the mother's womb (Ps. 139:13–18). Then think of the power that holds matter together, the power of God in sustaining the universe (Col. 1:17; Heb. 1:3), in maintaining the planets in their orbits, in preserving His creatures, and in answering prayer.

We see divine omnipotence in floods, fires, earthquakes, volcanic eruptions, storms, winds, and waves. We see it in the salvation of a sinner, in the healing of diseases, in the judgment of the wicked.

People measure power in megatons, the explosive force equivalent to that of a million tons of TNT. But human vocabulary has no word to adequately measure the power of God.

When the Old Testament saints thought of the power of God, they looked back to the Exodus when God delivered them from Egypt "with a mighty hand and with an outstretched arm" (Deut. 26:8).

In the New Testament, the greatest display of divine power was given in connection with the resurrection of Christ. Paul speaks of it as "the exceeding greatness of His power toward us who believe, according to the working of His mighty power which He worked in Christ when He raised Him from the dead and seated Him at His right hand in the heavenly places" (Eph. 1:19–20). It seems that Satan and all his hosts were encamped at the tomb outside Jerusalem, determined that the Lord Jesus would never rise. Then God came down in awesome power, drove back the armies of hell, and brought forth Christ in resurrection life. The whole scene is pictured vividly in Psalm 18:7–19.

It is sometimes taught that Jesus gave up His omnipotence when He came to earth. Or if He didn't give it up, He never used it. The idea is that He performed all His miracles by the power of the Holy Spirit.

I would admit that there were times when He chose not to use His power. For example, He could have destroyed His enemies at any time, but He had not come for that purpose. He had come to save, not to condemn. And besides, because He was morally perfect, He could not do anything that was contrary to His Father's will (John 5:19).

The fact that He performed miracles by the power of the Holy Spirit (Matt. 12:28) does not affect His omnipotence because at those very times He was sustaining the universe by the word of His power (Heb. 1:3).

At times He spoke of exercising His own power. He said, "Destroy this temple, and in three days *I will raise it up*" (John 2:19, emphasis added). Again, speaking of His death and resurrection, He said, "Therefore My Father loves Me, because I *lay down My life that I may take it again*. No one takes it from Me, but I lay it down of Myself. I have power to lay it down, and I have power to take it again" (John 10:17–18, emphasis added).

Jesus did not empty Himself of His omnipotence when He came to earth. It was hidden at times from human view, but it was always actively creating, sustaining, providing, guiding, and overruling.

Our hearts should be filled with worship and the fear of the Lord when we meditate on the omnipotence of our Lord. We are most apt to think of His *physical* power, but we must not overlook His *moral* power as well. E. Stanley Jones said, "The world is at the feet of the Man who had power to strike back, but who had power not to strike back. This is power—the ultimate power." He had power to summon more than twelve legions of angels, and yet the Omnipotent One could not save Himself if sinners were to be freed, as Albert Midlane pointed out:

> Himself He could not save,
> He on the cross must die,
> Or mercy cannot come
> To ruined sinners nigh;
> Yes, Christ, the Son of God, must bleed
> That sinners might from sin be freed.

There are very practical lessons to be learned from the omnipotence of God. The first lesson is that an individual cannot fight successfully against God. It would be like a gnat trying to fight against a blast furnace in a steel mill: "There is no wisdom or understanding or counsel against the LORD" (Prov. 21:30).

A second lesson is that those who are friends

of God are on the side of divine omnipotence and therefore are on the winning side. At any particular time the waves may seem to be against us, but the tide is sure to win. We need not fear what others can do to us. Nothing can happen to us apart from His permissive will. We believers are immortal until our work is done. God can control the emotions, intellect, and wills of our enemies so that they cannot touch a hair of our heads. In Exodus 34:23, God commanded all the males in Israel to attend the annual feasts in Jerusalem. But they would have left wives and children unprotected from enemy attacks. So God made an unusual promise in verse 24: "Neither will any man covet your land when you go up to appear before the LORD your God three times in the year." Only an omnipotent God could guarantee to control the wills of His foes.

Another lesson that we, as believers, must master is that we will never be omnipotent. We cannot share that attribute of God. But God has made His power available to us, at least in measure. We need not crawl when we can fly. If we live by our own strength, we will never rise above flesh and blood. But if we allow His Spirit to empower us, our lives will crackle with the supernatural.

Someone has said that people never come closer to omnipotence than when they pray in the name of the Lord Jesus. This testimony is true. When we pray in Jesus' name, it's the same as if the Lord Jesus was making the requests to the Father. With this realization, it's a wonder we don't pray more!

The final lesson that I will mention is that the omnipotence of God serves as comfort and encouragement to His people. What a consolation to know that our God can do anything, that nothing is impossible for Him! Oswald J. Smith reminds us that although *He* has no problems, He is able to cope with any problem *we* may be facing:

> The Savior can solve every problem,
> The tangles of life can undo.
> There's nothing too hard for Jesus;
> There's nothing that He cannot do.

Elisabeth Elliot tells of a motto on the wall of a China Inland Mission Home:

> The sun stood still. The iron did swim.
> This God is our God for ever and ever.
> He will be our guide unto death.

She comments,

This God, the one who, in answer to the prayers of an ordinary man, stopped the sun in its course, the God who suspended His own law of gravity and made an ax head float, this is the God to whom I come. This God is the one whose promises I am counting on. And can He help me out of my predicament? Whatever my

predicament may be, as soon as I compare it
with the circumstances surrounding the miracles
of the sun and the ax, my doubts seem comical.[3]

Mabel Brown Denison was moved to write
this verse:

> Great is our Lord; of great power.
> All things are upheld by His hand.
> The universe moves at His bidding,
> Or is stilled at His slightest command.

Isaac Watts proclaimed God's power:

> I sing the mighty pow'r of God
> That made the mountains rise,
> That spread the flowing seas abroad
> And built the lofty skies.
> I sing the wisdom that ordained
> The sun to rule the day;
> The moon shines full at His command,
> And all the stars obey.

Notes

1. *Omnipotent* and *almighty* are exact synonyms, one
from Latin and the other from Anglo-Saxon.

2. Stephen Charnock, *The Existence and Attributes of
God*, p. 364.

3. Elisabeth Elliot, *A Slow and Certain Light*, pp.
33–34.

— 7 —

In All Places
at All Times

Where can I go from Your Spirit?
Or where can I flee from Your
  presence?
If I ascend into heaven, You are there;
If I make my bed in hell, behold, You
  are there.
If I take the wings of the morning,
And dwell in the uttermost parts of the
  sea,
Even there Your hand shall lead me,
And Your right hand shall hold me.

—Psalm 139:7–10

God is omnipresent. He is present in all places at once. He fills heaven and earth.

In Jeremiah 23:23–24, we hear the Lord saying,

> Am I a God near at hand, . . .
> And not a God afar off?
> Can anyone hide himself in secret places,
> So I shall not see him? . . .
> Do I not fill heaven and earth?

Then there is this familiar verse: "For where two or three are gathered together in My name, I am there in the midst of them" (Matt. 18:20).

These are but two of the Scriptures that teach us that God is everywhere at one and the same time. He is ubiquitous (pervasive) and He is inescapable.

However, the omnipresence of God is not the same as pantheism. The latter equates God with things, with forces, and with laws. Pantheism (from *pan,* "all," and *theism,* "God") says that God is in the tree out in your yard; therefore, worship that tree. Another form of pantheism says that there are many gods, and they are all to be worshiped. Omnipresence applies only to the one true God. It says that He cannot be confined to any geographical location. He is everywhere, and people cannot hide from His presence.

An atheist once chalked on a wall, "God is nowhere." A child came along and, by inserting a space, changed it to read, "God is now here." John Arrowsmith told of a non-Christian philosopher who asked, "Where is God?" The Christian answered, "Let me first ask you, where is He not?"[1]

Thomas Watson wrote, "God's center is everywhere, His circumference nowhere."[2] And George Swinnock added, "God is neither shut up in nor shut out of any place."[3]

Although God is present everywhere, He is not apparent everywhere. Sometimes His presence is more manifest than at other times. Sometimes, as the poet Robert Lowell put it, "Behind the dim unknown, standeth God within the shadow, keeping watch above his own." But whether we discern Him or not, the fact remains: He is there.

When we remember that the Lord Jesus is God incarnate, we face the problem, Was He omnipresent during His ministry on earth? Did He not limit Himself to one location at a time—whether Bethlehem, Nazareth, Capernaum, or Jerusalem? The answer is a paradox. At the same time He was in any of these places, He was omnipresent. He did not lay aside His omnipresence when He came into the world. Rather, He took to Himself the added feature of being bodily present in only one locale. Thus, He could be in one place and heal a person in another (Matt. 8:13). He could be on earth and still be "in the bosom of the Father" (John 1:18). He could assure the disciples that He was always with them (Matt. 28:20), even though He knew that they would be scattered to different places (John 16:32).

Our minds obviously have trouble trying to reconcile these irreconcilables, but as the great French mathematician Pascal said, "The heart has its reasons which reason does not know."[4] And so does faith!

The doctrine of God's omnipresence cannot help affecting our lives. For instance, we cannot hide from God. Jonah tried to hide by taking a ship to Tarshish, but the Lord was waiting for him in the belly of a great fish.

Rebelling against his Christian background, a young man left Ireland for the United States. He later testified that Christ was waiting at the pier when he landed in New York. He was converted soon after. In his best-loved poem, the English poet Francis Thompson describes his futile effort to flee from the One he called "The Hound of Heaven":

I fled Him, down the nights and down the days;
I fled Him, down the arches of the years;
I fled Him, down the labyrinthine ways
Of my own mind, and in the midst of tears
I hid from Him, and under running laughter.[5]

At least, he tried to hide from Him! But like so many others, he found it was impossible. God was there when Thompson became exhausted with his flight.

But there's another side to the truth. Although the omnipresence of God serves as a warning to the world in general, it is also a wonderful comfort to His people. No matter what their circumstances may be, He is with them. I have had people ask me, "Where was God when the concentration camps were going on?" My answer was, "God was suffering with His people in the camps." When they go through the fire and flood, He is with them. He never leaves those He loves. They are never alone.

The fact that God is omnipresent should motivate me to live in holiness. He is there in the darkness of night. He is there where no human eye can see. He is there when I am away from home and loved ones. Whatever I do, I should ask myself, How does it appear in His presence? That is the true test for all our conduct. Listen to the words of H. C. Fish on this subject:

> How from Thy presence should I go,
> Or whither from Thy Spirit flee,
> Since all above, around, below,
> Exist in Thine immensity?
> If up to heaven I take my way,
> I meet Thee in eternal day.

Notes

1. The *Golden Treasury of Puritan Quotations,* compiled by I. D. E. Thomas, p. 120.

2. Ibid., p. 119.

3. Ibid.

4. The play on the word *reason* is in Pascal's original French: "Le coeur a ses *raisons* que la *raison* ne connaît point."

5. Francis Thompson, *Poetical Works,* p. 89.

– 8 –

The Eternal King

LORD, You have been our dwelling
place in all generations.
Before the mountains were brought
forth,
Or ever You had formed the earth and
the world,
Even from everlasting to everlasting,
You are God.

—Psalm 90:1–2

God is without beginning (Ps. 93:2) or end (Deut. 32:40; Ps. 102:27). He always existed and always will exist (Rev. 4:9–10). Therefore, it is correct to say that eternity is the lifetime of God. Our minds strain to take in the idea of an uncreated Being. We want to ask, Who made God? But the concept of God's eternity is too great for us to comprehend. He never had a beginning and will never have an end. He transcends time.

God's eternity is "duration without beginning or end; existence without bonds or dimensions; present without past or future. God's eternity is youth without infancy or old age; life without birth or death; today without yesterday or tomorrow."[1]

He is an eternal King (Ps. 10:16; 1 Tim. 1:17), who reigns forever (Pss. 66:7; 146:10) over an everlasting kingdom (Dan. 4:3, 34) from an eternal throne (Lam. 5:19).

Abraham was the first to describe Him as "the Everlasting God" (Gen. 21:33).

Moses spoke of the eternity of God: "The *eternal* God is your refuge, and underneath are the *everlasting* arms" (Deut. 33:27, emphasis added).[2]

Elihu added his praise:

> Behold, God is great, and we
> do not know Him;
> Nor can the number of His
> years be discovered (Job 36:26).

And David said of Him, "The LORD shall endure forever" (Ps. 9:7).

Isaiah spoke of the Lord as "Everlasting Father" (Isa. 9:6), and Daniel called Him "the Ancient of Days" (Dan. 7:9, 13, 22).

Habakkuk plaintively asked God, "Are You not from everlasting?" (Hab. 1:12).

Paul mentioned "the everlasting God" (Rom. 16:26).

The writer of the epistle to the Hebrews quoted God the Father as saying to His Son, "You remain . . . and Your years will not fail" (Heb. 1:11–12).

God does not live in the realm of time, but He uses the language of time to accommodate Himself to our understanding: "A thousand years in Your sight are like yesterday when it is past, and like a watch in the night" (Ps. 90:4). Peter reminds us that "with the Lord one day is as a thousand years, and a thousand years as one day" (2 Pet. 3:8). The Lord does not reckon time as we do. One writer observes,

> Events matter more to God than does the time during which they take place. In His Word, for example, God more or less ignores the 400 years which separated the burden of Malachi from the birth of Jesus. Yet He has devoted over 25 chapters to the events of the week in which our Lord died. God does not view or reckon time as we do. Still less is He governed or constrained by it as we are.[3]

Thoughts of the eternity of God should bow us in worship. As we push our minds back to the beginningless beginning and hurl them forward to His endless existence, we wonder and adore. As we realize that before there was anyone else and anything else, the Trinity was there—Father, Son, and Holy Spirit—we are lost in love and praise.

Contemplation of the eternity of God teaches us by contrast how short-lived we are here on earth. It causes us to pray, "So teach us to number our days, that we may gain a heart of wisdom" (Ps. 90:12). There are things we can do for God on earth that we'll never be able to do in heaven. We should be doing the works of the One who sent us while it is day because "the night is coming when no one can work" (John 9:4).

No wonder David prayed,

LORD, make me to know my end,
And what is the measure of my days,
That I may know how frail I am.
Indeed, You have made my days as handbreadths,
And my age is as nothing before You;
Certainly every man at his best
  state is but vapor (Ps. 39:4–5).

Isaac Watts declared,

Before the hills in order stood,
Or earth received her frame,
From everlasting Thou art God,
To endless years the same.

Notes

1. Quoted by William Evans in *The Great Doctrines of the Bible*, p. 35.

2. Our words *eternal* and *everlasting* are synonymous and, in the New Testament, translate the same Greek word (*aiōnios*).

3. M. Horlock, "The Eternal God," p. 127.

9

God Cannot Die

Now to the King eternal, immortal, invisible, to God who alone is wise, be honor and glory forever and ever. Amen.

—1 Timothy 1:17

God is not only *eternal,* He is *immortal* as well. The two words are often used interchangeably, but actually, there is a difference of meaning. As we have seen, God is eternal because He is without beginning or end of life. But He is immortal because He is not subject to death.

The Lord Jesus is immortal. Paul speaks of Him as the One "who alone has immortality, dwelling in unapproachable light" (1 Tim. 6:16). It was He "who has abolished death and brought life and immortality to light through the gospel" (2 Tim. 1:10). All three persons of the

Godhead are immortal. They are the source of deathlessness. They have the quality inherently, but they can bestow it on others.

The word *incorruptible* is also used of the Lord. It is not exactly the same as immortal, but it is closely related. It means "not subject to decay or corruption." Paul describes pagan man as changing "the glory of the incorruptible God into an image made like corruptible man" (Rom. 1:23), that is, exchanging worship of the living eternal God for a lifeless idol that would decay.

I stated that God cannot die. And yet the Lord Jesus Christ, who is God, died. He "was made a little lower than the angels, for the suffering of death . . . that He, by the grace of God, might taste death for everyone" (Heb. 2:9). It would be easy to get around the difficulty by saying that He died as far as His human nature is concerned but that as God He could not die. However, this answer is not satisfactory. We must not try to explain the paradox by separating the divine and human natures of the Lord. The two natures are inseparable. It is best just to leave the paradox as it is. God cannot die; Jesus is God; and yet Jesus died.

The bodies of believers, as of all people at the present time, are mortal and corruptible. The spirits and souls of believers are immortal. When Christ comes, believers will receive glorified bodies, which will be both immortal and incorruptible (1 Cor. 15:50–54). Then mortality will be "swallowed up by life" (2 Cor. 5:4). W. E. Vine points out that this latter expression shows that immortal "means more than deathlessness, it suggests the quality of the life enjoyed." And W. Chalmers Smith declares,

> Immortal, invisible, God only wise,
> In light inaccessible hid from our eyes,
> Most blessed, most glorious, the Ancient of Days,
> Almighty, victorious, Thy great name we praise.

— 10 —

Beyond Measure

But will God indeed dwell on the earth?
Behold, heaven and the heaven of heav-
ens cannot contain You. How much less
this temple which I have built!

—1 Kings 8:27

God is infinite. There is no way to measure or calculate His greatness. He is unbounded and limitless. No created intelligence can take it in. His greatness is inconceivable.

In Jeremiah 23:24, the Lord Himself rhetorically asks, "Do I not fill heaven and earth?"

Brother Lawrence, the author of the well-known *Practice of the Presence of God,* wrote,

To worship God in truth is to recognize . . . that God is what He is; that is to say, infinitely perfect, infinitely to be adored, infinitely removed from evil, and thus with every attribute divine. What man shall there be, however small the reason he may have, who will not use all his strength to render to this great God His reverence and worship?[1]

This may sound like a contradiction, but while God is infinite in all His attributes, there are limits to some of them. I have already mentioned that although He is omnipotent, He cannot do anything evil. In other words, His power is bounded by His holiness. Also, it should be noted that His mercy is not inexhaustible. His Spirit will not strive with sinners forever (Gen. 6:3). So no one should presume on the Lord.

When we think of God's infinity, it is good for us to remember how finite we are. The Scriptures compare us to such transient things as vapor, grass, flowers, wind, a weaver's shuttle, and a handbreadth. One day we're strong and healthy. Then a microscopic virus enters our systems, and soon we're as weak as a wet dishcloth. How wonderful that the infinite One should look down on us with great compassion, remembering that we are made of dust! He is worthy of all that we are and have.

Finally, although we may acknowledge that God is infinite, it is all too possible for us to assign limits to His ability. Israel did that in the wilderness: "Yes, again and again they tempted God, and limited the Holy One of Israel" (Ps.

78:41). In spite of all the miracles that He had performed for them, they quickly forgot and doubted His wisdom, love, and power. Such doubt is always an insult to His infinity. Lucy Ann Bennett had only praise for God's infinity:

> O Infinite Redeemer!
> I bring no other plea,
> Because Thou dost invite me,
> I cast myself on Thee.
> Because Thou dost accept me,
> I love and I adore;
> Because Thy love constraineth,
> I'll praise Thee evermore!

Note

1. Quoted by D. C. Egner in *Our Daily Bread,* March 6, 1983.

— 11 —

The Sovereign Ruler

For His dominion is an everlasting
*   dominion,*
And His kingdom is from generation
*   to generation.*
All the inhabitants of the earth are
*   reputed as nothing;*
He does according to His will in the
*   army of heaven*
And among the inhabitants of the
*   earth.*
No one can restrain His hand
Or say to Him,
"What have You done?"
                              —Daniel 4:34–35

The opening quotation is especially appropriate because of who wrote it and when. Its author was Nebuchadnezzar, the absolute monarch and sovereign of the Babylonian Empire. The time was the end of his humbling by God due to his arrogant pride. Even that Gentile king understood that the Lord is supreme in heaven and on earth, and cannot be hindered or held accountable to anyone.

Yes, our God is sovereign; He is the Supreme Ruler of the universe. As the One who is in complete charge, He can do as He pleases, and what He pleases is always good, acceptable, and perfect. To put it very simply, the doctrine of the sovereignty of God allows God to be God and refuses steadfastly to try to bring Him down to our level. He is over all and can do what He wants without explanation, permission, or apology.

We read of His sovereignty in Ephesians 1:11: "In Him also we have obtained an inheritance, being predestined according to the purpose of Him who works all things according to the counsel of His will." That last clause is pivotal— "who works all things according to the counsel of His will." That says God does as He pleases.

Isaiah pictures the Lord as

> declaring the end from the beginning,
> And from ancient times things
>   that are not yet done,

> Saying, "My counsel shall stand,
> And I will do all My pleasure" (Isa. 46:10).

Here God is claiming nothing less than supreme authority.

Absolute sovereignty would not be safe in the hands of anyone but God. As long as He exercises it, there is no danger of tyranny or despotism.

For believers, it is a wonderful thing to know that God is over all. It is a source of great comfort to know that we are not the victims of blind chance but that we are under His control. If the Supreme Ruler is on our side, no one can oppose us successfully (Rom. 8:31).

The sensitive English poet William Cowper teaches us to take fresh courage from the truth of God's supremacy:

> God moves in a mysterious way,
> His wonders to perform.
> He plants His footsteps in the sea,
> And rides upon the storm.
>
> Ye fearful saints, fresh courage take.
> The clouds ye so much dread
> Are rich with mercy and will break
> In blessing on your head.

The sovereignty of God is an appropriate theme of worship. Nothing could be more fitting than that we prostrate ourselves before Him in homage, praise, and thanksgiving for this wonderful attribute. J. Sidlow Baxter gives us a worshipful meditation on the sovereignty of the Son of God:

> The marvel which staggered Isaiah was that the despised, rejected, humiliated, bruised, wounded, pierced, broken, unresisting, meek and lowly, suffering Sin-bearer whom he saw "led as a lamb to the slaughter" was the very One whom he had earlier seen surrounded by overwhelming heavenly splendor, sitting on the glory-flashing throne, reigning in super-sovereignty over all nations and centuries! His omnipotent sovereignty which could crush a million alpha-stars underfoot and never feel them; that sovereignty with its blaze of sin-consuming holiness which could burn up the whole race of human sinners in instantaneous extinction; that eternal sovereignty which governs all worlds and all beings; *that* sovereignty incarnates itself in the person of *Jesus,* descends from that ineffable throne of glory, and hangs on that gory, felon's Cross as the *Lamb* which bears away the sin of the world![1]

And if the Lord is the Supreme Ruler, it is only right that we should submit ourselves to His control. He is the Potter and we are the clay. It would be ridiculous for the clay to question the Potter or to resist the pressure of His hand. The only reasonable response is, "Mold me and make me after Thy will, while I am waiting, yielded and still."

Some people have trouble with God's sovereign election, that is, with the fact that He has chosen certain individuals in Christ before the foundation of the world (Eph. 1:4). They find it hard to reconcile this with the many Scriptures teaching that whosoever will may come. The fact is that the Bible teaches sovereign election *and* human responsibility. The truth lies not somewhere between but in both extremes. They are parallel truths that meet only in infinity. The human mind cannot reconcile election and man's free will, but we believe both because the Bible teaches both. Any problem lies in our minds, not in God's.

The fact that God has chosen some to be saved does not mean that He has chosen the rest to be lost. The world is already lost and dead in sins. If left to ourselves, all of us would be condemned eternally. The question is, Does God have a right to stoop down, take a handful of already doomed clay, and fashion a vessel of beauty out of it? Of course He does. C. R. Erdman put it in right perspective when he said, "God's sovereignty is never exercised in condemning men who ought to be saved, but rather it has resulted in the salvation of men who ought to be lost."[2]

The only way people can know if they are among the elect is by trusting Jesus Christ as Lord and Savior (1 Thess. 1:4–7). God holds people responsible to accept the Savior by an act of the will. In reproving those Jews who did not believe, Jesus placed the blame on their will. He did *not* say, "You cannot come to Me because you are not chosen." Rather, He *did* say, "You *are not willing* to come to Me that you may have life" (John 5:40, emphasis added).

The real question of a believer is not, Does the sovereign God have the right to choose people to be saved? Rather, it is, Why did He choose *me?* This should make a person a worshiper for all eternity.

Another question sometimes arises in connection with God's sovereignty: Why did He allow sin? If He is the Supreme Ruler, why did He permit all the havoc that has come as a result of His creatures' lawlessness? Perhaps the following is at least part of the answer:

In deciding to create angels and human beings who had freedom of choice, God necessarily faced the possibility that they would rebel against Him. Of course, He could have created them without free choice. He could have made them like robots, bowing down to Him every hour on the hour. But it brings more glory to God to have His creatures love and worship Him because they want to.

As we know, Satan decided to rebel against God in heaven, and then he disobeyed Him on earth, bringing in a great flood of sickness, pain, tragedy, and death. But God is neither defeated nor outwitted. He set in motion the whole wonderful plan of redemption. As a result of Christ's finished work on the cross, more glory has come to God and more blessing to believers than if Adam had never sinned. We are better off in Christ than we ever could have been in an unfallen Adam. As someone has put it, "In Christ the sons of Adam boast more blessings than their father lost." Thus, God always has the last word. If sin enters His perfect creation, He is not frustrated by it but superabounds over it.

Sovereignty is a lovely attribute of God. Don't ever be afraid of it. Rest in it. Enjoy it. Worship Him for it. And allow Him to be God, saying with this anonymous poet:

> Reigning, guiding, all-commanding, ruling
> myriad worlds of light;
> Now exalting, now abasing, none can stay Thy
> hand of might!
> Yet we see Thy power and wisdom in Thy
> sovereign grace unite.

Notes

1. J. Sidlow Baxter, *The Master Theme of the Bible: Grateful Studies in the Comprehensive Saviorhood of Our Lord Jesus Christ,* p. 80.

2. Charles R. Erdman, *The Epistle of Paul to the Romans,* p. 109.

— 12 —
Far Above All

For thus says the High and Lofty One
Who inhabits eternity,
  whose name is Holy:
"I dwell in the high and holy place,
With him who has a contrite and
  humble spirit."

—Isaiah 57:15

God is exalted far above the universe. He alone is eternal, infinite, self-existent, self-sufficient, immutable, all-powerful, all-knowing, and all-present. These attributes place Him beyond the limits of material existence. He has His being apart from His creation:

Yours, O LORD, is the greatness,
The power and the glory,

The victory and the majesty;
For all that is in heaven and in earth is Yours;
Yours is the kingdom, O LORD,
And You are exalted as head over all.
Both riches and honor come from You,
And You reign over all.
In Your hand is power and might;
In Your hand it is to make great
And to give strength to all (1 Chron. 29:11–12).

O LORD God of our fathers, are You not God in heaven, and do You not rule over all the kingdoms of the nations, and in Your hand is there not power and might, so that no one is able to withstand You? (2 Chron. 20:6).

We see the transcendence of God in the way He not only overrules sin but also harnesses it to accomplish His own purposes. He allowed Satan and his agents to crucify the Lord of glory, yet by that death He doomed Satan and brought salvation to untold millions (Acts 2:23; 1 Cor. 2:8).

He allowed Job to suffer more loss than anyone else has suffered in one day, yet He vindicated His own name, silenced the devil, rewarded Job with double, and left succeeding generations a book that comforts them immeasurably in times of adversity.

He allowed Joseph's brothers to sell him into Egypt, yet He raised up Joseph to be the savior of his people. They meant evil against their brother, "but God meant if for good . . . to save many people alive" (Gen. 50:20).

When Jesus healed the man who was born blind, the religious leaders excommunicated him from the synagogue (John 9:34). Eventually, Jesus would have led him out of the fold of Judaism (John 10:3). So all they succeeded in doing was what the Lord Jesus would have done anyway.

Enemies of the gospel threw Paul into prison, yet from that prison came letters[1] that are now an important part of the inspired Word of God.

A proper appreciation of the Lord's transcendence will save us from entertaining small thoughts of God. It will save us from His rebuke: "You thought that I was altogether like you" (Ps. 50:21). And it will also save us from Luther's rebuke to Erasmus, "*Your thoughts of God are too human.*"

The shallow faith of our day can be attributed in great measure to the fact that believers have low views of God. We have failed to dwell in the secret place of the Most High, and we have failed to study the moral excellencies of the Lord. This has led to conceit and ignorance whereby we have exalted ourselves and our achievements, forgetting that we have nothing and can do nothing unless it is given to us from above. Our theology has become self-centered instead of God-centered.

Says Malcolm Davis,

> On a practical level, the truth of God's transcendence encourages an unquestioning faith to obey the Word of God at all times (even when there is no evidence of its fulfillment and positive discouragement from doing it), in the conviction that He will fulfill and reward obedience to it in His own time and way. It also engenders a patient humility to accept joyfully all God's dealings with us, even in trials, misunderstandings, and persecutions, although we do not understand the reason for them at the time; we simply trust that He will ultimately vindicate, and bless us as His people for His own Name's sake.[2]

We do ourselves a great disservice when we neglect the study of our transcendent God and His superlative virtues.

God the Son, who before the Incarnation was transcendent in glory, came down to this earth, to the very depths, as a slave who died the ignominious death of the cross (Phil. 2:5–11). But when His work was finished, He rose from the dead, ascended to heaven, and now sits transcendent on the Father's throne. A poet with the initials H. E. G. wrote,

> Far above all! far above all!
> Jesus the Crucified, far above all.
> Low at His footstool, adoring we fall.
> God has exalted Him far above all.

Notes

1. The Prison Epistles: Ephesians, Philippians, Colossians, and Philemon.
2. "The Transcendence of God," p. 76.

— 13 —

Too Great to Fully Comprehend

*Can you search out the deep things of
   God?*
*Can you find out the limits of the
   Almighty?*
*They are higher than heaven—what
   can you do?*
*Deeper than Sheol—what can you
   know?*
Their measure is longer than the earth
And broader than the sea.

            —Job 11:7–9

God is greater than our minds can take in. He is greater than the finest intellects, greater than human reasonings at their best. He cannot be fathomed by any created being.

Stephen Charnock said, "It is visible *that* God is. It is invisible *what* He is." And Richard Baxter observed, "You may know God, but not comprehend Him."

We may know what God has chosen to reveal of Himself in creation, in providence, in conscience, in redemption, in the Bible, and supremely in the person of Christ. Although no one has seen God at any time, yet "the only begotten Son, who is in the bosom of the Father, He has declared[1] Him" (John 1:18). So perfectly has the Son revealed the Father that He could say, "He who has seen Me has seen the Father" (John 14:9).

If we could fully comprehend God, we would be as great as He is. If He were a graven idol, we would be greater because we could design and manufacture Him. If He were a mere man, we could understand Him because we would be His equals. Even if He were an angel, He would not be beyond our comprehension because He, too, would be a created being.

But how can we comprehend a God who had no beginning, who has all power, all knowledge, all wisdom, and who is everywhere at once?

How can we understand one God existing in three equal persons—Father, Son, and Holy Spirit? Or how can we understand the mystery of the Incarnation—how the Lord Jesus Christ can be fully God and fully man?

And while we cannot understand Him, we can and must have the deepest reverence for Him. We must stand in awe as we think of His inscrutability. We must sing and love and wonder as we contemplate His fathomless majesty. And we must clothe ourselves with proper humility when we realize how shallow and transparent we are by comparison! Many years ago, Josiah Conder captured this idea:

> But the high myst'ries of His Name
> The creature's grasp transcend;
> The Father only (glorious claim!)
> The Son can comprehend.
> Worthy, O Lamb of God art Thou,
> That ev'ry knee to Thee should bow!

Note

1. The word translated "declared" originally meant "lead out." Our word for a careful expounding of the meaning of a biblical passage, *exegesis,* comes from this verb. The idea is drawing forth and declaring or expressing the content or truth about something or, here, Someone.

— 14 —

Perfect Foreknowledge

You only have I known of all the families of the earth.

—Amos 3:2

God is speaking in this verse to disobedient Israel. Obviously, God knows all the nations of history in the ordinary sense of that word, so *know* must have a deeper meaning. In the Old Testament, the Hebrew verb *know*[1] often suggests an intimate knowledge (such as Adam's knowing Eve), personal involvement, and choice (here, His electing Israel). Hebrew has no compound words such as *fore-know* or *pre-destine,* but Greek, Latin, and English do.

The words *foreknow* and *foreknowledge* suggest more than merely "knowing ahead of time." If God were not sovereign, He could never be sure what might happen. But He is sovereign. He knows what will happen because it is part of His will and plan. In the New Testament, God's foreknowledge or preplanning is used in connection with the Lord Jesus, with Israel, and with believers.

Concerning our Savior, we read, "Him, being delivered by the determined purpose and foreknowledge of God, you have taken by lawless hands, have crucified, and put to death" (Acts 2:23); and "He indeed was foreordained [foreknown, NASB] before the foundation of the world, but was manifest in these last times for you" (1 Pet. 1:20).

In what sense was Christ foreknown[2] by God? Was it simply that God had prior knowledge of what He would do, or did God's foreknowledge plan and determine what the Lord Jesus would do? Surely, it is the latter.

Concerning Israel, Paul writes, "God has not cast away His people whom He foreknew" (Rom. 11:2). Here the divine foreknowledge could not have been based on the mere prescience[3] of Israel's obedience because Israel was not obedient! Rather, God's foreknowledge was a sovereign choice of Israel as His earthly people.

Finally, concerning believers, we read, "For whom He foreknew, He also predestined to be conformed to the image of His Son, that He might be the firstborn among many brethren"

(Rom. 8:29); and "Elect according to the fore-knowledge of God the Father" (1 Pet. 1:2).

Regarding God's choosing or electing sinners in these last two verses, there are two main interpretations. One is that in eternity past God knew certain individuals in the sense that He sovereignly decided to bless them. The other view is that God knew beforehand those who would trust Christ as Lord and Savior, and His choice of them was based on this foreknowledge. The first view emphasizes the sovereignty of God in the matter of salvation, although it does not exclude the necessity of individuals responding to the gospel call. The second view emphasizes people's responsibility and makes God's choice of certain individuals dependent on their repentance and faith.

Whichever view we believe to be biblical, we should hold two truths in balance. First, God is sovereign, and He has the right to choose whomever He wishes, entirely apart from any merit on anyone's part. Second, God makes a bona fide offer of salvation to all the world, and people cannot be saved unless they put their faith in the Lord Jesus Christ. We cannot reconcile these two truths in this life, but it is essential that we hold them in balance.

The fact that God foreknows our eternal welfare should give us great thoughts about the Lord and lead us to praise Him. It should cause us to wonder why He ever looked on us with grace or favor. It should deliver us from pride when we remember that that favor was not prompted by any good in us.

An anonymous author penned these words:

> I sought the Lord, and afterward I knew
> He moved my soul to seek Him, seeking me;
> It was not I that found, O Saviour true;
> No, I was found of Thee.
>
> I find, I walk, I love; but O the whole
> Of love is but my answer, Lord, to Thee!
> For Thou wert long beforehand with my soul;
> Always Thou lovedst me.

Notes

1. Hebrew, *yādāh.*

2. The Greek word *proginōskō* literally equals "fore-know" (NASB), but KJV, NKJV and Charles B. Williams take the correct meaning to be "foreordain" (cf. "appoint," William F. Beck).

3. Merely knowing ahead of time without determining what will happen is called *prescience* (from Latin for "preknow").

— 15 —

Always the Same

For I am the LORD, I do not change.

—Malachi 3:6

God is immutable. He does not change in His being, His attributes, or His purpose. He is the unchanging One, the same yesterday, today, and forever.

In Psalm 102:24, the Messiah prays from the cross, "O my God, do not take me away in the midst of my days." The Father replies,

Your years are throughout all generations.
Of old You laid the foundation of the earth,
And the heavens are the work of Your hands.
They will perish, but You will endure;
Yes, they will all grow old like a garment;
Like a cloak You will change them,
And they will be changed.

But You are the same,
And Your years will have no end (vv. 24–27).

Those words, "You are the same," describe the immutability of the Lord. Creation will be changed, but He knows no change.

Another verse that deals with God's immutability is this one: "The Father of lights, with whom there is no variation or shadow of turning" (James 1:17). In J. N. Darby's translation of Isaiah 37:16, "the Same" is rendered as a name of God: "Thou, the Same, thou alone art the God of all the kingdoms of the earth." This name is also found in Isaiah 41:4.

However, while it is true that God does not change in His being, He does use different methods. In the history of the human race, He has tested people under various conditions, whether under innocence, conscience, promise, law, or grace. In different dispensations, He has tested people with regard to sin and responsibility, although the way of salvation has always been the same, that is, by grace through faith. This does not affect His immutability at all.

Neither does the fact that God is said to "repent" (KJV) or "relent" (NKJV) affect His immutability. Here we come up against what might seem to be a contradiction. On the one hand, we read, "God is not a man, that He should lie, nor a son of man, that He should repent" (Num. 23:19); and "The

Strength of Israel will not lie nor relent" (1 Sam. 15:29). Yet we also read, "And the LORD was sorry that He had made man on the earth" (Gen. 6:6); and "I greatly regret that I have set up Saul as king" (1 Sam. 15:11). How can God be immutable and still repent or relent? The answer is simply this. By His very nature, He must reward obedience and punish disobedience. As long as His creatures obey Him, He blesses them. But if they embark on a life of sin, He has no choice but to discipline them. Therefore, God's "repentance" is a change in His purposes and plans toward those whose character and conduct have changed. It seems like repentance to us; therefore, we might call it the language of human appearance. It certainly doesn't mean that the change in people has taken God by surprise or that He is acting out of regret, resentment, or irritation. It simply means that what we think of as repenting or relenting is necessary in order for God to act consistently with His character.

We must not think of the immutability of God merely as dry doctrine. Its truth should speak immeasurable comfort to our souls. We live in a world of change and decay. It's wonderful to have a God who is changeless. We ourselves change from day to day, but we can look to One who is always the same. We can depend on Him to be unchangeable and faithful in all His dealings with us.

Even though immutability is a unique characteristic of God, we should still be imitators of

Him to the extent that believing persons can be. In other words, we should not be fickle, moody, or vacillating. We should not be Dr. Jekyll one day and Mr. Hyde the next. We should not be kind, gracious, and outgoing to strangers but ill-mannered to our families! We should be not only willing but even anxious to change where improvement or progress is indicated. On the other hand, we should be unchanging when it comes to standing for what is right.

The beloved hymn "Abide with Me" by Henry F. Lyte contrasts God's immutability with the mutability of all else:

> Swift to its close ebbs out life's little day,
> Earth's joys grow dim, its glories pass away;
> Change and decay in all around I see—
> O Thou who changest not, abide with me!

Part Two

Shared Attributes of God

As children copy their fathers, you, as God's children, are to copy Him.

—From Paul's Letter to the Ephesians (5:1 PHILLIPS)

— 16 —

God Is Spirit

God is Spirit, and those who worship Him must worship in spirit and truth.

—John 4:24

When we say that God is Spirit, we mean that He is a spiritual Being who does not dwell in a material body. We are so used to thinking of persons in relation to bodies that it is difficult for us to imagine anyone living without a body. But angels do not have a body except on those rare occasions when they appear in human guise. And we will live without a body after death (2 Cor. 5:8; Phil. 1:23)—at least until the resurrection of the just.[1]

The fact that God is Spirit does not deny His personality. He is a Person with intellect, emotions, and will—the components of personhood.

Because God is Spirit, He is invisible to mortal eyes (Col. 1:15; 1 Tim. 6:16). However, in Old Testament times, He manifested His presence in the shekinah or glory cloud. He also made Himself visible as the Angel of Jehovah, generally believed to be the Lord Jesus in a preincarnate appearance.

In the New Testament, God became visible in the person of the Lord Jesus Christ. Thus, we read, "No one has seen God at any time. The only begotten Son, who is in the bosom of the Father, He has declared Him" (John 1:18). And later Jesus said, "He who has seen Me has seen the Father" (John 14:9).

Whenever God appears to people, His glory is veiled. It would be impossible for unredeemed humanity to look on God's unveiled glory and live. Jacob was surprised that he survived after seeing God (Gen. 32:30). And yet the Savior promised that the pure in heart will see God (Matt. 5:8).

That brings us to the inevitable question, If God is Spirit and therefore invisible, will we see God in heaven? The simplest answer is that Jesus is God, and we will certainly see Jesus in heaven.

But perhaps there is more. In heaven the limitations of this earthly body will be set aside. We will have powers that we cannot imagine now. Although we cannot see God with these mortal eyes, is it not possible that, as one youngster suggested, we will have bigger eyes in heaven? We cannot be wrong in claiming the absolute promise of the Lord Jesus: "Blessed are the pure in heart, for *they shall see God*" (Matt. 5:8, emphasis added).

The fact that God is Spirit has practical lessons for us. In speaking to the woman of Samaria, the Lord Jesus said, "God is Spirit, and those who worship Him must worship in spirit and truth" (John 4:24). Her thoughts of worship centered on a tangible temple on a visible mountain (Gerizim) with material aids to devotion. Jesus told her that "the hour is coming, and now is, when the true worshipers will worship the Father in spirit and truth; for the Father is seeking such to worship Him" (John 4:23).

True worship is not confined to any place or building on earth. It is not concerned with stained-glass windows, ecclesiastical garments, candles, liturgies, or incense. Rather, in genuine worship we pass from earth to heaven by faith, and there, in the presence of God, we pour out our souls in thanksgiving, praise, and homage to the Lord for all He is and for all He has done for us.

One other duty emerges from the fact that God is Spirit and therefore invisible. It is found by comparing John 1:18 and 1 John 4:12. In John 1:18, we read, "No one has seen God at any time. The only begotten Son, who is in the bosom of the Father, He has declared Him." In other words, when Christ was on earth, He showed the world what God is like. Then in 1 John 4:12, we read, "No one has seen God at any time. If we love one another, God abides in us, and His love has been perfected in us." Here the thought is that it is now our responsibility to show the world what God is like. The Savior is no longer bodily present in the world. But when we love one another, God dwells in us, and the world gets a practical demonstration of the invisible God. Ours is an awesome responsibility:

God, Thou art Spirit, glorious and majestic,
We love Thee, Lord, though Thee we cannot see.
Before Thy royal throne, of Thy grace now trophies,
In spirit and in truth, we now worship Thee.

Note

1. Some Bible scholars believe that Christians will have an intermediate body between death and the resurrection to a glorified body.

Wonderful Love

God is love.

—1 John 4:16

God's love is His tender affection for others and His deep concern for their good. It involves a strong emotional attachment and a commitment that manifests itself in giving. Thus, we read that "God so loved the world that He gave His only begotten Son" (John 3:16), and "Christ . . . loved the church and gave Himself for her" (Eph. 5:25). When we read that "God is love," we are reading a description, not a definition. We do not worship love, but we worship the God who is love.

J. I. Packer defines God's love as "an exercise of His goodness towards individual sinners whereby, having identified Himself with their welfare, He has given His Son to be their Savior, and now brings them to know and enjoy Him in a covenant relation."[1]

But however hard we may try to define it, we need an enlarged, improved vocabulary. Our present dictionary is not adequate. There are not enough adjectives—simple, comparative, and superlative. Our language is utterly impoverished. Individual words are ashamed. We can go only so far; then we have to say, "The half has not been told." The subject exhausts all human language. Let us begin, then, on a theme that cannot be finished.

God's love is eternal, the only love that is unoriginated. It is age-abiding and unending. Our minds strain to comprehend a love that is ceaseless and unremitting.

It is immeasurable. Its height, depth, length, and breadth are infinite. Nowhere do we find such extravagance. Poets have compared it to creation's greatest expanses, but the words always seem to break under the weight of the idea.

His love to us is causeless and unprovoked. The great God could see nothing lovable or meritorious in us to draw out His affections, yet He loved us just the same. That's the way He is.

Our love of others is often based on ignorance. We love people because we don't really know what they are like. The more we get to know them, the more we become aware of their faults and failures, and then the less likable they

appear. But God loves us even though He knew
all that we would ever be or do. His omniscience
did not cancel His love.

But there are so many people in the world—
more than five billion. Can the Sovereign love
each one personally? As one poet asked,

> Among so many, can He care?
> Can special love be everywhere?

Yes, with Him there are *no* nobodies. No one
is insignificant. His affection flows out to every
individual on the planet.

Such love is incomparable. Many people have
known the love of a devoted mother. Or the
faithful love of a selfless spouse. David knew the
love of Jonathan. And Jesus knew the love of
John. But no one has ever experienced anything
that can compare with the divine love. As a
hymn reminds us, "No one ever cared for me
like Jesus."

In Romans 8, Paul ransacks the universe for
anything that might separate the believer from
God's love, but he comes up empty. Not death,
life, angels, principalities, powers, things present
or to come, height, depth, or any created thing
can divorce the believer from God's love.

It is awesome to realize that the omnipotent
God cannot love you or me more than He does

at this moment. It is the same love that He showers on His unique Son, and it is absolutely unrestrained and unreserved.

In a world of constant flux, it is assuring to find something that is unchanging, namely, the love of God. Our love moves in cycles. It is an emotional roller coaster. Not so with our Lord. His love never tires or varies.

And it is pure love, utterly free from selfishness, unrighteous compromise, or unworthy motive. It is untainted and without a breath of defilement.

Like His grace, God's love is free. For this we can be everlastingly thankful because we are paupers, beggars, and bankrupt sinners. And even if we owned all the wealth in the world, we still could never put a down payment on a love so priceless.

Here is love that is wonderfully impartial. It causes the sun to shine on the just and the unjust. It orders the rain to fall without discrimination.

And perhaps the most amazing thing about it is that it is sacrificial. It led the holy Son of God to Calvary to give its greatest demonstration. H. Rossier put it this way:

> Lord, e'en to death Thy love could go,
> A death of shame and loss,
> To vanquish for us every foe
> And break the strong man's force.

At the cross we see a love that is stronger than death, that not even the billows of God's wrath could drown.

This unique love surpasses knowledge and defies the powers of utterance. It is sublime and matchless, the Everest of all affection.

We may search the earth for a better dictionary, a larger vocabulary to describe the Lord's love. But it is all in vain. Not until we reach heaven and gaze on incarnate Love will we see with clearer vision and understand with keener intellect the love of God that is in Christ Jesus our Lord. Hasten the day, O blessed Lord Jesus!

No wonder the writers of Scripture speak so often of this favorite attribute:

> The LORD did not set His love on you nor choose you because you were more in number than any other people . . . but because the LORD loves you (Deut. 7:7–8).

> Yes, I have loved you with an
>   everlasting love;
> Therefore with lovingkindness
>   I have drawn you (Jer. 31:3).

> He will quiet you with His love,
> He will rejoice over you with singing (Zeph. 3:17).

> As the Father loved Me, I also have loved you; abide in My love (John 15:9).

The love of God has been poured out in our hearts by the Holy Spirit who was given to us (Rom. 5:5).

But God demonstrates His own love toward us, in that while we were still sinners, Christ died for us (Rom. 5:8).

The Son of God, who loved me and gave Himself for me (Gal. 2:20).

His great love with which He loved us (Eph. 2:4).

By this we know love, because He laid down His life for us (1 John 3:16).

In this the love of God was manifested toward us, that God has sent His only begotten Son into the world, that we might live through Him. In this is love, not that we loved God, but that He loved us and sent His Son to be the propitiation for our sins (1 John 4:9–10).

To Him who loved us and washed us from our sins in His own blood (Rev. 1:5).

The love of God is a subject that can never be exhausted. No human mind will ever be able to fathom it. The poet was right when he said that if all the oceans were ink, the sky one enormous stretch of parchment, every blade of grass a pen, and every person a writer—"to write the love of God above would drain the ocean dry, nor would the scroll contain the whole, though stretched from sky to sky."

The Lord's love makes us think of Him as our Friend—the Friend who is closer than a brother—the Friend who loves at all times—the Friend of publicans and sinners. What a Friend we have in Jesus!

No subject should awaken greater thoughts of worship in our hearts. It is overwhelming to think that God loves each one of us in a personal, intimate way, and that He sent the Son of His love to die as our sacrificial substitute on the cross of Calvary. It is amazing that His love will not be completely satisfied until He has us all with Him in heaven for all eternity.

Think of all the hymns and poems that have been composed in praise of the love of God, the books that have been written, the messages that have been preached. And yet that is not enough. God's will is that His love be manifested in our lives! The world today is dying for lack of love, and only Christians can really fill the need.

How, then, can we imitate God in this pearl of perfections?

John suggests two ways—being willing to lay down our lives for fellow believers, and sharing our material possessions with those who are in need (1 John 3:16–17). But there are other ways. Love sees things to be done and does them without being asked. Love doesn't keep a count of wrongs. Love gives without any thought of return. John Oxenham expressed it in verse:

> Love ever gives, forgives, outlives,
> And ever stands with open hands;
> And while it lives it gives,
> For this is love's prerogative—
> To give, and give, and give.[2]

It goes out to the last, the least, and the lowest:

> Love has a hem to its garment
> That reaches right down to the dust.
> It can reach the stains of the streets and lanes,
> And because it can, it must.
>
> It dare not rest on the mountain;
> It must go down to the vale;
> For it cannot find its fullness of mind
> Till it kindles the lives that fail.[3]

We should never lose a sense of wonder that God's love for us is so undeserved. The language of our hearts should be:

> How Thou canst love me as Thou dost
> And be the God Thou art
> Is darkness to my intellect
> But sunshine to my heart.[4]

We should love Him with a love that is undivided, obedient, and worshipful, allowing no rival to share the throne with Him.

We should love our brothers and sisters in Christ without regard to denominations or religious labels. John insists that if we do not love our brothers whom we have seen, we cannot love God whom we have not seen (1 John 4:20).

And we should love the world of unredeemed men and women, ever praying,

> Let me look on the crowd as my Savior did
> Till my eyes with tears grow dim.
> Let me view with pity the wand'ring sheep
> And love them for love of Him.[5]

In this poem the apostle Paul voices his passion for souls:

> Only like souls I see the folk thereunder,
> Bound who should conquer, slaves who should be
> kings
> Hearing their one hope with an empty wonder,
> Sadly contented with a show of things.
>
> Then with a rush the intolerable craving
> Shivers throughout me like a trumpet call,
> O to save these, to perish for their saving,
> Die for their life, be offered for them all.[6]

When this is our spiritual craving, we are getting close to Calvary love. Dave Hunt states,

> God's love toward mankind is not some impersonal cosmic force that operates inexorably by a universal law, but is intensely personal. God loves each of us with a passion. We find that incredible fact extremely difficult to believe, much less to understand. We look within ourselves to find the *reason* for His love. Yet it would not be comforting if God loved us because we somehow deserved or had aroused His love, because we could change and lose that appeal and thus lose His affection. It is, instead, assuring to know that He loves us *because of who He is in Himself*—and *in spite of* who and what we are. Since God *is* love and since He never changes, we are secure for eternity and need never fear that we could lose His love by anything we might do or neglect to do.[7]

The Irish hymn writer Thomas Kelly says it well:

> "God is love!" His Word has said it;
> This is news of heavenly birth:
> Speed abroad and widely spread it,
> Make it known through all the earth
> That "God is love."

Notes

1. J. I. Packer, *Knowing God,* p. 136.
2. John Oxenham. 1852–1941. By permission of Desmond Dunkerley.
3. Source and author unknown.
4. Source and author unknown.
5. Source and author unknown.
6. Source and author unknown.
7. Dave Hunt, *Global Peace,* pp. 246–48.

— 18 —

Amazing Grace

The LORD is gracious and full of compassion.

—Psalm 111:4

God grants acceptance to those who don't deserve it, who, in fact, deserve the very opposite, but who trust the sinner's Savior. This is grace! It is the gift of heaven's Best for earth's worst. It is *God's Riches At Christ's Expense.*

God's grace is sovereign. That means it is of the most exalted kind and bestowed according to God's good pleasure. He did not have to save any of us. J. I. Packer writes, "Only when it is seen that what decides each man's destiny is whether or not God resolves to save him from his sins, and that this is a decision which God need not make in any single case, can one begin to grasp the biblical view of grace."[1]

Grace is unmerited. There is nothing in sinful

men and women to draw it forth. On the contrary, if they received justice, they would perish eternally. It is not merely that fallen men and women have a total lack of merit; they have accumulated an enormous load of positive demerit.

Grace is a free gift. It is something that cannot be bought. It cannot be earned by good character or good works. Any idea of achieving God's favor by joining a church, keeping the sacraments, giving to charity, obeying the Ten Commandments, or living by the golden rule is ruled out. If we could earn it or deserve it, that would be debt, not grace, as Paul pointed out in Romans 4:4–5: "Now to him who works, the wages are not counted as grace but as debt. But to him who does not work but believes on Him who justifies the ungodly, his faith is accounted for righteousness."

Archbishop Temple said, "The only thing of my own which I contribute to my redemption is the sin from which I require to be redeemed."

Grace is abounding. It is greater than all our sins, flowing as a mighty tide from Calvary, sufficient for everyone but efficient only for those who receive it.

God can offer His grace to the lost because of Christ's work on Calvary. By His substitutionary death and resurrection, the Lord Jesus fully satisfied the claims of divine justice and fully paid the debt that our sins deserved. God can righteously justify the ungodly when they receive the Savior by faith. And when they receive Him, they receive all the benefits of His atoning work.

Left to themselves, sinful men and women do not want to be recipients of divine grace. It wounds their pride to think that they cannot save themselves by their character or works. In their independence of God, they resent being welfare or charity cases. They want to think that there is something they can do or be to deserve heaven. But no one can ever be saved who is not willing to be infinitely in debt.

Not only do fallen men and women not want God to show grace to them; they do not like to see God showing grace to others. They are like the Pharisees, to whom Jesus said, "You shut up the kingdom of God against men; for you neither go in yourselves, nor do you allow those who are entering to go in" (Matt. 23:13).

No attribute of God is greater than another. They are all perfect. Yet somehow the grace of God has appealed to believers as chief in the galaxy of divine excellencies. In prose and poetry, it has earned a favorite place. For example, Samuel Davies wrote,

> Great God of wonders! All Thy ways
> Display Thine attributes divine;
> But the bright glories of Thy grace
> Above Thine other wonders shine,

> Who is a pard'ning God like Thee?
> Or who has grace so rich and free?

God has always been a God of grace—in the
Old Testament as well as in the New. But that
aspect of His character was revealed in a new
and arresting way with the coming of Christ.

Grace is a golden thread that goes through the
New Testament. It was part of Paul's customary
salutation ("Grace and peace"). He frequently
extolled the grace that not only saved him but
called him as a servant of God.

Here are some of the principal Bible passages
dealing with grace:

And the Word became flesh and dwelt among
us, and we beheld His glory, the glory as of the
only begotten of the Father, full of grace and
truth. . . . And of His fullness we have all received, and grace for grace (John 1:14, 16).

For the law was given through Moses, but grace
and truth came through Jesus Christ (John
1:17).

Being justified freely by His grace through the
redemption that is in Christ Jesus (Rom. 3:24).

For sin shall not have dominion over you, for you
are not under law but under grace (Rom. 6:14).

For you know the grace of our Lord Jesus
Christ, that though He was rich, yet for your
sakes He became poor, that you through His
poverty might become rich (2 Cor. 8:9).

My grace is sufficient for you, for My strength is made perfect in weakness (2 Cor. 12:9).

I do not set aside the grace of God; for if righteousness comes through the law, then Christ died in vain (Gal. 2:21).

For by grace you have been saved through faith, and that not of yourselves; it is the gift of God, not of works, lest anyone should boast (Eph. 2:8–9).

For the grace of God that brings salvation has appeared to all men (Titus 2:11).

But may the God of all grace, who called us to His eternal glory by Christ Jesus, after you have suffered a while, perfect, establish, strengthen, and settle you (1 Pet. 5:10).

It was sovereign grace that chose us in Christ before the foundation of the world; we will never know why He chose us. It was wonderful grace that sent the Son of God to this planet to become a man. It was amazing grace that led the Lord Jesus to Calvary's cross to die on our behalf.

Grace saved us from the penalty of sin—an eternity of horror in hell. Grace redeemed us from the slave market of sin. Grace reconciled us to God. By grace we are justified, sanctified, and glorified. What was it but grace that caused us to be indwelt by the Holy Spirit, who is the guarantee of our eternal security and the pledge that the full inheritance will one day be ours?

Marvelous grace made us children of God, heirs of God, and joint heirs with Jesus Christ. The moment we are saved we are blessed with all spiritual blessings in the heavenlies—matchless tokens of the grace of God. And His grace will never be fully satisfied until we are in glory with Christ and conformed to His blessed image. No wonder J. N. Darby asked,

> And is it so—I shall be like Thy Son?
> Is this the grace which He for me has won?
> Father of glory (thought beyond all thought!),
> In glory, to His own blest likeness brought!

If we see that salvation is all of grace, we can have full assurance. We can know that we are saved. If salvation depended in the slightest degree on ourselves and on our miserable attainments, we could never know for sure that we were saved. We wouldn't know whether we had done enough good works or the right kind. But when salvation depends on the work of Christ, there doesn't have to be any nagging doubt.

The same is true of our eternal security. If our continued safety somehow depended on our ability to hold out, we might be saved today and lost tomorrow. But as long as our safety depends entirely on the Savior's ability to keep us, we can know we are eternally secure.

Those who live under law are helpless pawns

of sin because law tells them what to do but doesn't give them the power to do it. Grace gives people a perfect standing before God, teaches them to walk worthily of their calling, enables them to do it by the indwelling Holy Spirit, and rewards them for doing it.

Under grace, service becomes a joyful privilege, not a legal duty. Believers are motivated by love, not by fear. The memory of what the Savior suffered to provide salvation inspires saved sinners to pour out their lives in devoted service.

The charge is often made that the teaching of salvation by grace alone encourages sin: "If you are saved by grace, you can go out and live the way you please." The truth is that a true appreciation of the grace of God provides the strongest motivation for holy living. People will do out of love what they would never do out of fear of punishment. Was that not what Augustine meant when he said, "Love [God] and do what you will"?

Once we receive the grace of God, we become worshipers forever. Each of us asks, Why should He have chosen me? Why should the Lord Jesus have shed His life's blood for one so unworthy? Why should God not only save me from hell but bless me with all spiritual blessings in the heavenlies now and destine me to spend eternity with Him in heaven?

Of course, God wants His grace to be reproduced in our lives and to flow through us to others. He wants us to be gracious in our dealings with others. Our "speech" should "always be with grace, seasoned with salt" (Col. 4:6). We should impoverish ourselves that others might be enriched (2 Cor. 8:9). We should show favor and acceptance to the unworthy and the unlovely.

If we are to truly represent our Lord and Savior, we must exhibit the same grace that characterized Him in His life on earth. August M. Toplady proclaimed,

'Twas grace that wrote my name in life's eternal book;
'Twas grace that gave me to the Lamb, who all my sorrows took.
Saved by grace alone! This is all my plea:
Jesus died for all mankind, and Jesus died for me.

O let Thy grace inspire my soul with strength divine:
May all my powers to Thee aspire, and all my days be Thine.
Saved by grace alone! This is all my plea:
Jesus died for all mankind, and Jesus died for me.

Note

1. J. I. Packer, *Knowing God*, p. 146.

— 19 —

Rich in Mercy

His mercy endures forever.

—Psalm 136 (twenty-six times)

Closely related to the grace of God is His mercy. Whereas His grace pours out blessings we don't deserve, His mercy withholds punishment we do deserve. His mercy is the pity, lovingkindness, and compassion He shows to those who are in misery and distress. His mercy causes the sun to shine on the just and the unjust. In the King James tradition, *mercy* is often synonymous with *lovingkindness*.[1]

Here are some verses that speak of God's mercy:

The LORD, the LORD God, merciful and gracious, longsuffering, and abounding in goodness and truth, keeping mercy for thousands, forgiving iniquity and transgression and sin, by no means clearing the guilty (Exod. 34:6–7).

Surely goodness and mercy shall follow me
All the days of my life (Ps. 23:6).

For the LORD is good;
His mercy is everlasting,
And His truth endures to all generations (Ps. 100:5).

Blessed be the God and Father of our Lord Jesus Christ, the Father of mercies and God of all comfort (2 Cor. 1:3).

But God, who is rich in mercy (Eph. 2:4).

The Lord is very compassionate and merciful (James 5:11).

Mercy and truth united at the cross of Calvary, and by this union atonement is provided and iniquity is purged (Prov. 16:6). Thomas Kelly expressed it poetically:

> Mercy and truth unite;
> O 'tis a wondrous sight, all sights above!
> Jesus the curse sustains,
> Guilt's bitter cup He drains,
> Nothing for us remains, nothing but love!

When people asked the Lord for mercy for sick relatives, they meant the mercy of healing. When blind people asked the Lord for mercy, they meant the mercy of sight. When Paul wrote, "Grace, mercy, and peace," to Timothy and others, he meant the sympathetic concern of God for weak and failing servants. When Jude said that we should be "looking for the mercy of our Lord Jesus Christ unto eternal life" (Jude 21), he was referring to Christ's coming for His saints.

When I read a verse like Ephesians 2:4, I feel I have discovered God's roadblock on one's way to hell—"But God, who is rich in mercy." He is so rich in mercy that none need perish, but individuals must come to God in His appointed way. I adore the mercy that had lovingkindness, pity, and compassion on me. And I praise Him for the mercies of life—for sight, hearing, smell, memory, appetite, soundness of body and mind, food, drink, and all the wonders of nature.

As always, privilege brings responsibility. God wants us to imitate Him in this quality of mercy. He wants us to be merciful to one another: "Therefore be merciful, just as your Father also is merciful" (Luke 6:36).

Let me give you a modern illustration of mercy in action. One day, a Christian named Paul went into a coffee shop, sat on a stool, and ordered his lunch. When he began speaking to the man next to him, he realized that Fred was in deep spiritual need. After sharing the gospel with him, Paul arranged to meet him again. It was at the second meeting that Fred was converted. Then

Paul began to disciple him on a one-on-one basis, and Fred grew in grace and in the knowledge of the Lord Jesus. But it wasn't long before Fred learned that he had a life-threatening disease. He had to go to a convalescent hospital that was sadly substandard. Paul visited him regularly, bathed him, changed the sheets, and did other chores that the staff should have been doing. The night Fred died, Paul was holding him in his arms, whispering verses of Scripture in his ear. That's mercy. It's a wonderful thing to see that Godlike quality in a human life.

The apostle Paul exhorts us to show mercy with cheerfulness (Rom. 12:8). A Christian woman once explained the verse to me in an unforgettable manner. She said, "I had an aged mother who was living alone, but the time came when she couldn't handle it any longer. I talked to my husband, and we decided to bring her to our house. Deep within my heart I was reluctant and resentful. It disturbed the routine of our home and threw many of my plans for a loop. I cared for her. I cooked her meals. I did her laundry. I did everything for her. But my mother would say to me, 'Why don't you smile anymore? You don't seem to be your former happy self!' You see, I was showing mercy, but I wasn't doing it with cheerfulness."

When Jesus said, "I desire mercy and not sacrifice" (Matt. 9:13), He taught that it is more important for us to show a loving, helpful concern for others than to bring Him the most costly offering. He is interested not in ritual but in reality.

It is not surprising that one of the beatitudes deals with this noble virtue: "Blessed are the merciful, for they shall obtain mercy" (Matt. 5:7). If we want mercy, we have to show it. John Milton penned these words:

> Let us, with a gladsome mind,
> Praise the Lord, for He is kind:
> For His mercies shall endure.
> Ever faithful, ever sure.
>
> He hath with a piteous eye,
> Looked upon our misery:
> For His mercies shall endure,
> Ever faithful, ever sure.

Note

1. In the KJV and NKJV both *mercy* and *lovingkindness* are used to translate the same Hebrew word *hesed* (rhymes with *blessed*).

— 20 —

Fearful Wrath

For the wrath of God is revealed from heaven against all ungodliness and unrighteousness of men, who suppress the truth in unrighteousness.

—Romans 1:18

The wrath of God is His righteous indignation and fury against sin and unrepentant sinners. Although we would rather think of His love, mercy, and grace, God's wrath is as much a divine perfection as any of His other attributes: "It is not the ignoble outburst that human anger so often is, a sign of pride and weakness, but it is holiness reacting to evil in a way that is morally right and glorious."[1]

At various times in human history, God has revealed His anger against sin. He sent the Flood to destroy the world of Noah's day. He consumed Sodom, Gomorrah, and the cities of the plain with fire and brimstone. He caused the ground to open and swallow Korah, Dathan, and Abiram. The isolated exhibitions of wrath were designed to show succeeding generations God's displeasure with specific sins and with sin in general. Fortunately for us all, He does not blaze out against every occurrence of sin.

God's wrath will be revealed during the Tribulation period when the seals are opened, the trumpets are blown, and the bowls of His fury are poured out on a world that rejected His Son.[2] And it will be revealed when the Lord Jesus returns to earth as King of kings and Lord of lords, when God breaks His silence and pours out His wrath:

> It shall thunder with the force of offended righteousness, strike with lightning bolts upon the seared consciences; roar as the long-crouched lion upon dallying prey; leap upon, batter, destroy and utterly consume the vain reasonings of proud human kind; ring as the battle shout of a strong, triumphant, victory-tasting warrior; strike terror and gravity to souls more forcefully than tortured screams in the dead of night. O God, what shall be the first tones of that voice again on earth? And what their effect? Wonder and fear, denizens of dust, for the Lord Himself shall descend from heaven with a battlecry, with the voice of the archangel and the trumpet blast of God Himself, made more terrible, if that could be, by the longsuffering of His silence.[3]

God's wrath is revealed in Hades and in the lake of fire, which is the same as hell. Hades is the temporary prison of the unsaved dead, a place of conscious suffering. At the judgment of the great white throne, death and Hades, that is, the bodies, souls, and spirits of the unsaved, will be cast into the lake of fire. Jesus, quoting Isaiah 66:24 three times for emphasis, described the final and eternal abode of the unsaved as a place "where 'their worm does not die, and the fire is not quenched' " (Mark 9:44, 46, 48). And John wrote, "The smoke of their torment ascends forever and ever" (Rev. 14:11).

There is another place where the wrath of God is revealed—that is at the cross of Calvary. There the concentrated indignation of God was poured out on His beloved Son when He bore our sins in His body. The Savior endured the agonies of hell for three hours—the hell that we should have endured for all eternity. It was not only physical suffering but also the indescribable horror of being forsaken by God. There is no way that we can ever fathom the extent of His suffering. G. W. Frazer writes,

> The depth of all Thy suffering
> No heart could e'er conceive;
> The cup of wrath o'erflowing
> For us Thou didst receive.

Some key references to God's wrath are the following ones:

> If I whet My glittering sword, and My hand takes hold on judgment, I will render vengeance to My enemies, and repay those who hate Me (Deut. 32:41).

God is jealous, and the LORD avenges;
The LORD avenges and is furious.
The LORD will take vengeance on His adversaries,
And He reserves wrath for His enemies;
The LORD is slow to anger and great in power,
And will not at all acquit the wicked.
The LORD has His way
In the whirlwind and in the storm,
And the clouds are the dust of His feet.
He rebukes the sea and makes it dry,
And dries up all the rivers.
Bashan and Carmel wither,
And the flower of Lebanon wilts.
The mountains quake before Him,
The hills melt,
And the earth heaves at His presence,
Yes, the world and all who dwell in it.
Who can stand before His indignation?
And who can endure the fierceness of His anger?
His fury is poured out like fire,
And the rocks are thrown down by Him.
The LORD is good,
A stronghold in the day of trouble;
And He knows those who trust in Him.

But with an overflowing flood
He will make an utter end of its place,
And darkness will pursue His enemies (Nah. 1:2–8).

He who believes in the Son has everlasting life;
and he who does not believe the Son shall not
see life, but the wrath of God abides on him
(John 3:36).

What if God, wanting to show His wrath and to
make His power known, endured with much
longsuffering the vessels of wrath prepared for
destruction? (Rom. 9:22).

Let no one deceive you with empty words, for
because of these things the wrath of God comes
upon the sons of disobedience (Eph. 5:6).

In flaming fire taking vengeance on those who
do not know God, and on those who do not
obey the gospel of our Lord Jesus Christ. These
shall be punished with everlasting destruction
from the presence of the Lord and from the
glory of His power (2 Thess. 1:8–9).

Fall on us and hide us from the face of Him who
sits on the throne and from the wrath of the
Lamb! (Rev. 6:16).

He himself shall also drink of the wine of the
wrath of God, which is poured out full strength
into the cup of His indignation. He shall be tor-
mented with fire and brimstone in the presence
of the holy angels and in the presence of the
Lamb. And the smoke of their torment ascends
forever and ever; and they have no rest day or

night, who worship the beast and his image, and whoever receives the mark of his name (Rev. 14:10–11).

So the angel thrust his sickle into the earth and gathered the vine of the earth, and threw it into the great winepress of the wrath of God (Rev. 14:19).

Then one of the four living creatures gave to the seven angels seven golden bowls full of the wrath of God (Rev. 15:7).

Go and pour out the bowls of the wrath of God on the earth (Rev. 16:1).

He Himself treads the winepress of the fierceness and wrath of Almighty God (Rev. 19:15).

We often hear the charge that it would be improbable, if not impossible, for a God of love to sustain an everlasting hell. The wrath of God, they say, is incompatible with His mercy. Those who hold this bizarre notion should consider the following truths.

The Bible itself is emphatic and clear in setting forth wrath as one of God's attributes. A. W. Pink says that "there are more references in Scripture to the anger, fury and wrath of God than there are to his love and tenderness." Jesus spoke more of hell than of heaven. C. H. Spurgeon notes that we cannot neglect any of the attributes of God—not even wrath: "The terrible

Avenger is to be praised, as well as the loving Redeemer. Against this the sympathy of man's evil heart with sin rebels; it cries out for an effeminate God in whom pity has strangled justice. The well-instructed servants of Jehovah praise him in all the aspects of his character, whether terrible or tender."[4]

God, however, never intended hell for humankind; it was created for the devil and his angels (Matt. 25:41). Judgment is His strange work (Isa. 28:21).

No man or woman has to go to hell. God provided deliverance at enormous cost, but individuals must receive God's salvation by faith.

If a person refuses mercy, there is no alternative but wrath. If one doesn't want to go to heaven on God's terms, there is no other place but hell. J. I. Packer correctly points out that

> the essence of God's action in wrath is to *give men what they choose,* in all its implications: nothing more, and equally nothing less. God's readiness to respect human choice to this extent may appear disconcerting and even terrifying, but it is plain that His attitude here is supremely just, and poles apart from the wanton and irresponsible inflicting of pain which is what we mean by cruelty.[5]

G. K. Chesterton, who was converted from atheism, said that "hell is the finest compliment that God could make to the dignity of human personality and to the freedom of man's choice."

There is no doubt that God is the most misunderstood and maligned person in the universe. He warns people against the consequences of sin. Then when they willfully disobey and bring themselves to ruin, they rage against the Lord. Men and women willfully do what God has forbidden, and then they blame God when the promised judgment falls. In longsuffering mercy, God provides a way of salvation, but unbelievers refuse it and go crashing over the precipice into hell, reviling God all the way.

If we are to imitate the virtues of God, what about this attitude of wrath? Is it ever right for believers to be wrathful? The answer is that a certain kind of anger is actually commanded: "Be angry, and do not sin" (Eph. 4:26). But there is always the danger of even righteous anger getting out of control, and so the verse goes on to say, "Do not let the sun go down on your wrath." We should be angry when God's name and cause are dishonored. Thus, Jesus was angry when the money changers made His Father's house a den of thieves. As someone has said, we should be lions in God's cause but lambs in our own.

Generally speaking, wrath isn't safe in our hands, so the Scriptures contain warnings:

Beloved, do not avenge yourselves, but rather give place to wrath; for it is written, "Vengeance is Mine, I will repay," says the Lord (Rom. 12:19).

Let all bitterness, wrath, anger, clamor, and evil speaking be put away from you, with all malice (Eph. 4:31).

So then, my beloved brethren, let every man be swift to hear, slow to speak, slow to wrath; for the wrath of man does not produce the righteousness of God (James 1:19–20).

It is cause for ceaseless worship that believers will never experience the wrath of God. They can say exultantly with Paul Gerhardt:

> There is no condemnation
> There is no hell for me.
> The torment and the fire
> My eyes shall never see.
> For me there is no sentence,
> For me death has no sting.
> Because the Lord who loves me
> Shall shield me with His wing.

But the contemplation of the wrath of God should give us compassion for the lost and a desire to see them fleeing to the arms of Jesus. We should pray, give, and go out in active evangelism to our relatives, neighbors, and friends.

Certainly, there is a warning here to the unconverted: "The wrath of God—not His vengefulness or anger, but that which makes Him *against* sinful man to the point of *giving up* man (Rom. 1:18, 24, 26, 28)! Think—the Supreme Power in the universe *against* what you are doing, determined that you shall fail! The Supreme Power leaving you to yourself in silent scorn."[6] The thought is terrible; the reality is worse, as Isaac Watts plainly stated:

> O dreadful hour! when God draws near,
> And sets men's crimes before their eyes!
> His Wrath their guilty souls shall tear,
> And no deliv'rer dare to rise.

Notes

1. J. I. Packer, *Knowing God,* p. 189.

2. See Revelation 6—19.

3. Elisabeth Elliot, quoting Jim Elliot in *Shadow of the Almighty,* p. 111.

4. Charles Haddon Spurgeon, *Treasury of David* 4:386.

5. Packer, *Knowing God,* p. 170.

6. Foreman, *Daily Notes of the Scripture Union.*

The Holy One

Holy, holy, holy is the LORD of hosts;
The whole earth is full of His glory!

—Isaiah 6:3

God is holy. His name is holy (Isa. 57:15), and as His name, so is He. That means He is morally perfect in His thoughts, deeds, and motives and in every other way. He is free from all sin and defilement, or as John puts it, "God is light and in Him is no darkness at all" (1 John 1:5). He cannot be more holy that He is. He is absolutely pure, immaculate, and spotless. A. W. Tozer writes, "Before the uncreated fire of God's holiness, angels veil their faces. Yea, the heavens are not clean, and the stars are not pure in His sight." God hates sin and is enraged by the slightest outbreak of it. He kept Moses out of the Promised Land for not treating Him as holy

(Num. 20:12). God's holiness distinguishes Him from all His creatures (Exod. 15:11).

The seventeenth-century English preacher Stephen Charnock pointed out that the word *holy* is used more often as a prefix to God's name than any other attribute. Two examples are "the Holy One" and "the Holy One of Israel."

The Bible has many passages that teach the holiness of God, but we will confine ourselves to three.

First is Leviticus 19:2: "You shall be holy, for I the LORD your God am holy." Actually, Leviticus 19 is one of the principal chapters on the subject. Over and over we hear Jehovah saying, "I am the LORD your God . . . I am holy . . . you shall be holy." We hear it echoed in 1 Peter 1:15–16.

Then in Habakkuk 1:12–13, the prophet says,

O LORD my God, my Holy One. . . .
You are of purer eyes than to behold evil,
And cannot look on wickedness.

That doesn't mean God can't see what's going on. He sees every sin that is ever committed. That means He cannot look on sin with any measure of approval. He cannot condone iniquity. He cannot countenance anything that's wrong.

The third verse is Revelation 4:8: "Holy, holy,

holy, Lord God Almighty, who was and is and is
to come!" The threefold use of the word *holy* is
not only repetition for emphasis; it also means
that the Lord is holy to the highest degree.[1]

Throughout the Old Testament period, God
taught the meaning of holiness through object
lessons. The priesthood, for instance, showed
that in order for sinful men and women to ap-
proach the holy God, they must come by way of
a mediator. The sacrificial system said, in effect,
that fallen men and women can draw near to the
thrice-holy God only with the blood of a sacrificial substitute. The temple ritual allowed only
one man of one race, one tribe, and one family
to enter the presence of God only on one day of
the year. The laws concerning marriage, cloth-
ing, clean and unclean foods, and ceremonial
washing proclaim that the holy God requires His
people to be holy.

Coming over to the New Testament, we actually see holiness embodied in a man, the God-
man, Christ Jesus. His was the only perfect life
ever lived on this earth. He knew no sin (2 Cor.
5:21). He did no sin (1 Pet. 2:22). There was no
sin in Him (1 John 3:5). He could say, "The ruler
of this world is coming, and he has nothing in
Me" (John 14:30). There was nothing in the sinless Savior to respond to the evil solicitations of
Satan. Even Pilate had to admit three times that
he found no fault in Jesus (John 18:38; 19:4, 6).

We get a tremendous glimpse of His holiness when we see Him in the Garden of Gethsemane. Calvary was drawing near. The Savior knew that He would soon identify Himself with all the sins of all the world. He knew that our sins would be laid on Him and that He would become a sin offering. The very thought of His coming into contact with sins in that way caused Him the keenest suffering. We read that "His sweat became like great drops of blood falling down to the ground" (Luke 22:44).

Here we see the difference between our sinful lives and Jesus' holy life. It causes us pain to resist temptation; it caused Him pain to contemplate it. We agonize when we decide not to sin; He agonized at the thought of contact with our sins.

But let us move on to Calvary in order to witness one of the greatest displays of God's holiness. The drama of redemption is about to take place. We know at the outset that God must punish sin. His holiness forbids Him to condone it, excuse it, or look the other way. But wait! The sacrificial victim is God's own beloved Son, who is there not because of any sins He committed but because of your sins and mine. What will God do now? Will He spare His Son? Will He make an exception in this case? Or will He pour out His unmitigated wrath on His sinless Son when He sees the Lord Jesus bearing our sins in His body on the tree? We know the answer. The holiness of God cannot be compromised. He unsheathes His sword and it strikes Christ. As Anne Ross Cousin phrased it,

> The tempest's awful voice was heard,
> O Christ, it broke on Thee;
> Thy open bosom was my ward;
> It bore the storm for me.
> Thy form was scarred, Thy visage marred;
> Now cloudless peace for me.

God's holiness never cost Him more dearly than at Calvary, but we can be eternally grateful that He was willing to pay the price. Major André gratefully declared,

> On Him [Christ] almighty vengeance fell,
> That must have doomed a world to hell;
> He bore it for a sinful race
> And thus became my hiding place.

George Cutting pointed out that "the gospel does not tell of a God whose love has been expressed in winking at sin, but of a God whose love to the sinner could only be expressed where His holy claims against sin were righteously met and its penalty exhaustively endured."[2]

Now what practical effects should the truth of God's holiness have on our lives? Every indicative (statement) in the Bible gradually becomes an imperative (command). In other words, doctrines are designed to affect not only our minds but also our whole lives. A person could fill the frontal lobes with theology and still be as cold as ice. It is not enough to know Christian truth; it must become flesh in us.

Contemplation of the holiness of God should produce in us a sense of reverential awe. We should remove our shoes because the place on which we stand is holy ground (Exod. 3:5):

> God is greatly to be feared in the
>   assembly of the saints,
> And to be held in reverence
>   by all those around Him (Ps. 89:7).

A. W. Tozer said, "Never forget that it is a privilege to wonder, to stand in delighted silence before the Supreme Mystery and whisper, 'O Lord God, Thou knowest.' " If we do that, we will never stoop to undue familiarity by speaking of God as a cosmic pal. Said Josh McDowell, "He may be your Father, but he's not your Dad."

When we see God's holiness, we should also see our own utter sinfulness. When Isaiah saw the Lord, he cried, "Woe is me, for I am undone! Because I am a man of unclean lips" (Isa. 6:5). When Job saw the Lord, he said, "I abhor myself, and repent in dust and ashes" (Job 42:6). When Peter saw the Lord, he cried, "Depart from me, for I am a sinful man, O Lord!"

(Luke 5:8). Julian of Norwich, a medieval English Christian, wrote, "The beholding and the loving of the Maker maketh the soul to seem less in his own sight, and most filleth him with reverent dread and true meekness; with plenty of charity for his fellow Christians."

The more we think of the holiness of God, the more we are inspired to worship Him. In a world of sin and moral pollution, we can turn away to One whose character is absolutely untainted. When oppressed with our unholiness, we can rejoice in One who is free from any failure or imperfection. We can praise Him that all the claims of holiness were met by the work of the Savior on the cross, and that now God can come out to us in love, grace, and mercy. Seraphim and cherubim veil their faces and prostrate themselves before the blinding light of His purity. How much more should we!

And then this glorious attribute of God should mold our everyday behavior. We should find sin to be increasingly revolting and should experience increasing longing for holiness. If we are going to walk in fellowship with God, we must put away sin and walk in the light. Nothing must be hidden under the counter. We must "pursue . . . holiness, without which no one will see the Lord" (Heb. 12:14). As Archbishop Temple put it, "No one is a believer who is not holy, and no one is holy who is not a believer."

Finally, if we have a proper appreciation of the holiness of God, it will save us from entertaining shallow views concerning the sinlessness of Christ. For instance, we often hear the perverse notion that Jesus could have sinned as a man, even if He never did. It is argued that otherwise His temptation in the wilderness would not have been real. Such a doctrine raises some disturbing questions. How could Jesus be God if He had anything less than the full attributes of God? If He could have sinned as a man here on earth, what is to prevent His sinning as a man in heaven? If He could have sinned, does that mean He was capable of committing murder, rape, fornication, and sodomy? The fact of the matter is that the Lord Jesus not only *did* not sin, He *could* not sin.[4] His humanity was perfect whereas ours is fallen. Like us, He could be tempted from without, but unlike us, He could not be tempted from within. Our Savior is holy, harmless, undefiled, and separate from sinners (Heb. 7:26). His holiness cannot be breached or compromised.

We read twice in Hebrews that the Lord Jesus was made perfect: "For it was fitting for Him, for whom are all things and by whom are all things, in bringing many sons to glory, to make the captain of their salvation perfect through sufferings" (Heb. 2:10); and "And having been perfected, He became the author of eternal salvation to all who obey Him" (Heb. 5:9).

However, these verses do not mean that Jesus was made perfect as far as His moral character was concerned. That would have been impossible because He was always perfect in His character, words, and works. But He was made perfect as our Savior. In order to bring salvation to us, He had to leave heaven, be incarnated as a man, suffer, bleed, and die. He could never have become our perfect Savior if He had remained in heaven. He had to suffer all the punishment that our sins deserved to become perfect as the Captain of our salvation.

There is none like Him: "Who is like You, O LORD . . . glorious in holiness, fearful in praises, doing wonders?" (Exod. 15:11). Reginald Heber understood that our God is holy:

Holy, Holy, Holy! All the saints adore Thee,
Casting down their golden crowns around the glassy sea;
Cherubim and seraphim falling down before Thee,
Which wert and art, and evermore shalt be.

Holy, Holy, Holy! Though the darkness hide Thee,
Though the eye of sinful man Thy glory may not see,
Only Thou art holy; there is none beside Thee
Perfect in power, in love, and purity.

Notes

1. In many ancient manuscripts of Revelation there is a ninefold repetition of the word, perhaps suggesting three for each person of the Trinity. See this verse in *The Greek New Testament According to the Majority Text* (Nashville: Thomas Nelson Publishers, 1982).

2. George Cutting, *Light for Anxious Souls,* p. 13.

3. Julian of Norwich, *Revelations of Divine Love,* pp. 14–15.

4. Theologians have used two little Latin phrases to contrast the true from the false view on this doctrine. The correct teaching is *non posse peccare* (not possible to sin); it is not merely *posse non peccare* (possible not to sin).

— 22 —

Wise Beyond Description

Oh, the depth of the riches both of the wisdom and knowledge of God! How unsearchable are His judgments and His ways past finding out!

—Romans 11:33

Another wonderful attribute of God is His wisdom. This is somewhat connected with His knowledge, but it is not the same. His knowledge speaks of His vast range of information and understanding, whereas His wisdom means His ability to use this knowledge to produce the best possible results by the best possible means. It is His perfect judgment and infallible insight:

With Him are wisdom and strength,
He has counsel and understanding. . . .

135

With Him are strength and prudence.
The deceived and the deceiver are His (Job 12:13,
  16).

O LORD, how manifold are Your works!
In wisdom You have made them all.
The earth is full of Your possessions (Ps. 104:24).

The LORD by wisdom founded the earth;
By understanding He established the heavens;
By His knowledge the depths
  were broken up,
And clouds drop down the dew (Prov. 3:19–20).

Traces of the wisdom of God can be seen in the natural creation, but the full revelation will stretch out through eternity. Take the universe, for instance. A recent scientific article said that it is so finely tuned that the odds of achieving it by chance "would be the same as throwing an imaginary microscopic dart across the universe to the most distant quasar and hitting a bull's-eye one millimeter in diameter."

The human body is a masterpiece of divine wisdom and engineering. For example, one writer observed, "The brain has been called an enchanted loom. Somehow it is able to take the shifting electric signals from 252 million rods and cones in [man's] eyes and, moment by moment, weave these tiny snippets of information into a tapestry portrait of what is before him."[1] Similarly, the DNA, which is the basis of heredity, "is so narrow and so compacted that all the genes in all my body's cells would fit into an ice cube; yet if the DNA were unwound and joined together end to end, the strand could stretch from the earth to the sun and back more than four hundred times."[2]

There is the miracle of the mind, concerning which its Designer asked,

> Who has put wisdom in the mind?
> Or who has given understanding
> to the heart? (Job 38:36).

There is the miracle of the spirit by which we can have fellowship with God. In prayer we leave planet earth, enter the throne room of the universe, and converse with the King.

God's wisdom is seen also in the spiritual creation. The plan of salvation demonstrates it. Paul reminds us that "since, in the wisdom of God, the world through wisdom did not know God, it pleased God through the foolishness of the message preached to save those who believe" (1 Cor. 1:21); and "Christ [is] the power of God and the wisdom of God" (1 Cor. 1:24). In His wisdom God did not choose the wise, mighty, and noble people; He chose the foolish, weak, base, despised—in short, nobodies—to bring glory to Himself (1 Cor. 1:26–29).

All creation is filled with evidence of divine wisdom. All His works express His wisdom.

The wisdom of God, perfect and complete, means that He can never make a mistake. As we sometimes say, He is too loving to be unkind, too wise to make a mistake. What confidence this gives us in the Lord! No matter what happens to us, it is neither an error nor an accident. We would plan our lives exactly the same way He planned them if we had His wisdom.

It means that His guidance is the best. We can trust His leading. Too often we take matters into our own hands. If we were wise, we would let Him choose for us. He is the truly wise Counselor.

It is true that we can never be as wise as God is, but that doesn't excuse us from drawing on His resources and exhibiting wisdom in our everyday lives. We are to be "wise as serpents and harmless as doves" (Matt. 10:16). We should be characterized by the wisdom that is from above, a wisdom that is pure, peaceable, gentle, easy to be entreated, "full of mercy and good fruits, without partiality and without hypocrisy" (James 3:17). We are wise if we hear the teachings of Jesus and do them (Matt. 7:24). We must walk in wisdom toward those who are outside the faith (Col. 4:5).

Believers reveal other features of true wisdom. We do not judge by outward appearances. We value the praise of God rather than the praise of people. We share God's view that the things that most people esteem are abominations. We learn from the Word of God and thus avoid a lot of bitter lessons in the school of experience. We find safety in a multitude of counselors. We find peace in accepting things in life that cannot be changed. In these and countless other ways, we believers manifest ourselves as persons of wisdom and true children of the One of whom Isaac Watts wrote,

> He formed the stars, those heavenly flames,
> He counts their numbers, calls their names:
> His wisdom's vast, and knows no bound,
> A deep where all our thoughts are drowned.

Notes

1. Lowell Ponte, "How Color Affects Your Moods," p. 95.

2. Dr. Paul Brand and Philip Yancey, *Fearfully and Wonderfully Made,* p. 46.

God Is Good

You are good, and do good.

—Psalm 119:68

God is good in the sense that He is morally perfect. All He does is good, that is, kind and beneficial. He is excellent and completely free from anything that is malicious or unworthy. He is merciful, gracious, generous, loving, patient, forgiving, and trustworthy—all these and more are included in His goodness.

David spoke of "the goodness of the LORD in the land of the living" (Ps. 27:13). He also said,

Oh, how great is Your goodness,
Which You have laid up for those who fear You,
Which You have prepared for
   those who trust in You
In the presence of the sons of men! (Ps. 31:19).

The earth is full of the goodness of the LORD
   (Ps. 33:5).

And all are invited to "taste and see that the
LORD is good" (Ps. 34:8). His goodness "endures continually" (Ps. 52:1). It is a frequent refrain in Scripture:

For the LORD is good;
His mercy is everlasting,
And His truth endures to all generations
   (Ps. 100:5).

The LORD is good to all,
And His tender mercies are over
   all His works (Ps. 145:9).

The LORD is good,
A stronghold in the day of trouble;
And He knows those who trust in Him (Nah. 1:7).

C. H. Spurgeon shows how God's goodness is
so fundamental to our faith:

"He is good." This is reason enough for giving
Him thanks; goodness is His essence and nature,
and therefore He is always to be praised whether
we are receiving anything from Him or not.
Those who only praise God because He *does*
them good should rise to a higher note and give
thanks to Him because He *is* good. In the truest
sense He alone is good. "There is none good but
one, that is God"; therefore in all gratitude the

Lord should have the royal portion. If others seem to be good, He *is* good. If others are good in a measure, He is good beyond measure. When others behave badly to us, it should only stir us up the more heartily to give thanks unto the Lord, because He is good; and when we ourselves are conscious that we are far from being good, we should only the more reverently bless Him that "He is good." We must never tolerate an instant's doubt as to the goodness of the Lord; whatever else may be questionable, this is absolutely certain, that Jehovah is good; His dispensations may vary, but His Name is always the same, and always good. It is not only that He was good, and will be good, but He *is* good; let His providence be what it may. Therefore, let us even at this present moment, though the skies be dark with clouds, yet give thanks unto His Name.[1]

God's goodness is seen in creation, providence, and redemption. Think of the beauty of creation—the mountains, lakes, trees, flowers, sunsets, stars, animals, birds, and fish. Think of the goodness of God in providence—how He feeds, protects, guides, cares for, and befriends all of His creation. And greatest of all, ponder His goodness in redemption—that He should send heaven's Best to die for earth's worst.

J. I. Packer points out that "God is good to all in some ways and to some in all ways." His common grace is shown to all in "creation, providence and all the blessings of this life." His

special grace is shown to believers in the blessings of salvation.

No wonder the psalmist said, "Oh, that men
would give thanks to the LORD for His goodness,
and for His wonderful works to the children of
men!" (Ps. 107:8). If we would only pause long
enough to ponder the many evidences of His
goodness in our lives, we would be more worshipful and grateful. The trouble is that we take
it all for granted and our hearts become cold
and unresponsive.

The contemplation of His goodness to us
should awaken in us a desire to be good to others—to be kind and benevolent and to be faithful friends. We can manifest goodness by being
tenderhearted, generous, forgiving, considerate,
gentle, and hospitable.

Someone might ask, "If God is so good, why
did He make the devil?" The answer is that God
created him as an angelic being who was perfect
in all his ways (Ezek. 28:15) but was a free
moral agent with power to obey or disobey God.
When this "son of the morning" sought to usurp
the throne of God, he fell from heaven (Isa.
14:12–15). It was not God's fault that His crea-
ture chose to rebel against Him.

Another questioner might ask, "If God is
good, why does it say that He originates evil,
sickness, suffering, tragedy, death, and so on?" In
Isaiah 45:7, for instance, we hear Him saying, "I

make peace and create evil" (KJV). Here the word *evil* means "adversity" or "calamity" (NKJV). But does God send calamity? It should be clearly understood that God is never the source of evil or of anything bad. Some Scriptures seem to indicate that He is, but the true explanation is that God is often said to do things that He only permits to be done. In other words, He allows His creatures, human and angelic, to do things that are not good, then He overrules these evil things for His glory and for the good of His people.

A third question that might arise is, "If God is good, why does He punish evil?" Stephen Charnock answered the question by asking, "How could God be a friend to goodness if He is not an enemy to evil?" It is a mark of goodness to punish evil. To let it go unchecked and unpunished would be a denial of all that is good. And John Greenleaf Whittier was reassured by God's goodness:

> Yet, in the maddening maze of things,
> And tossed by storm and flood,
> To one fixed trust my spirit clings:
> I know that God is good!

Note

1. Charles Haddon Spurgeon, *Treasury of the Bible* 5:320.

— 24 —

Unbounded Generosity

Trust . . . in the living God, who gives us richly all things to enjoy.

—1 Timothy 6:17

Yes, the Lord is incredibly generous. Too often we take His generosity for granted. We need to be constantly reminded that He gives us richly all things to enjoy.

Think of His generosity in the natural realm. He has provided us with two hundred fifty thousand different kinds of seed-bearing plants, of which fifty thousand are trees—evergreens, oaks, maples, willows, birches, and a host of others. These help to make our planet a place of tremendous beauty rather than a lunar landscape.

God created eighty-six hundred different flowers for our enjoyment. Take orchids alone; there are two thousand varieties. Solomon's glory did not compare with the magnificence of the scarlet wild anemones that grow in profusion on the hillsides of the Holy Land. There is no way to measure the pleasure that people have derived from roses, irises, lilies, carnations, daisies, begonias, African violets, and all the others.

We must not forget the fruit trees and berry bushes. Apples are a favorite wherever they are found. What can compare with the delight of sinking one's teeth into a tree-ripened Bartlett pear, having the juice flow down one's chin and reveling in the incomparable flavor? Not to mention peaches, bananas, oranges, grapes, plums, and cherries! And who can resist a slice of freshly baked blueberry pie, its juice collecting on the plate? Even the mention of raspberries and strawberries evokes similar pleasurable sensations.

There are ten thousand species of birds, every one a wonderful creation of God. We marvel at the tiny hummingbird that can cross the Gulf of Mexico without having to stop to refuel. We enjoy the peppy little English sparrow, scratching around for its daily food and leaving the future to its Creator. We ponder the migratory travels of many birds and marvel at the homing instinct of the pigeon.

It is estimated that there are twenty thousand kinds of bony fish and an additional ten thousand other kinds. Many of them are paragons of grace and beauty, and many supply us with food of exquisite flavor.

Vegetables add variety, color, and flavor to the ordinary meal—potatoes, carrots, lettuce, peas, beans, beets, and corn. The list is almost endless.

Without flavors and fragrances, life would be drab and monotonous. God made the chocolate flavor[1] and the fragrance of lilacs.

Our generous God spangled the heavens with stars, billions of which we will never see. Probably no science reveals the greatness of God more than astronomy, at the same time showing us our insignificance.

And what shall we say of the beauty of a sunset, the grandeur of the mountains, and the expanse of the seas? No human mind can begin to take in the magnitude or the variety of God's breathtaking creation.

No wonder the father of English hymnody, Isaac Watts, could sing,

> I sing the goodness of the Lord
> That filled the earth with food;
> He formed the creatures with His word
> And then pronounced them good.
> Lord, how Thy wonders are displayed
> Where'er I turn my eye:
> If I survey the ground I tread
> Or gaze upon the sky!

But while the Bible points to the lavishness of God in nature, it lays even greater emphasis on His generosity in the spiritual realm.

The psalmist reminds us that God's thoughts toward His people are more numerous than the sand of the sea (Ps. 139:18). If he had said more numerous than a handful of sand, that would have been astounding. But he said more numerous than all the sand of the sea.

God gives wisdom liberally to all who ask for it (James 1:5). In reading the Bible, we should watch for adverbs like that word *liberally,* for adjectives describing plenitude, and for verbs expressing lavishness.

Our Father "daily loads us with benefits" (Ps. 68:19). It is as if we are pressed down under the weight of blessings. What a wonderful burden!

The greatest display of God's generosity was when He gave His only begotten Son. When He emptied heaven of its choicest Treasure, when He sent heaven's Best for earth's worst, no gift could ever be greater than that!

We know the generosity of the Lord Jesus Christ in that, though He was rich, He voluntarily "became poor" for our sake that we "through His poverty might become rich" (2 Cor. 8:9). This is the example of generosity He left to us.

God is generous in grace. Where sin abounded, grace superabounded (Rom. 5:20). Paul described divine grace as exceedingly abundant

(1 Tim. 1:14). It is a mighty ocean. We stand at the shore with our little thimbles; we fill our thimbles, but the ocean is in no way depleted.

God is generous in mercy. If it were not so, we would have perished long ago. He did not mete out to us the punishment we deserved. We experience His mercy through all of life, and it continues to our children's children.

When we are born again, He pours out His Spirit on us abundantly (Titus 3:6). Involved in this outpouring are all the ministries of the Holy Spirit. How much we owe to them!

At the same time, these words of the Lord Jesus are fulfilled: "I have come that they may have life, and that they may have it more abundantly" (John 10:10).

Even when we are called to go through suffering and trial, consolations abound. They are sufficient for every tribulation (2 Cor. 1:5).

God supplies all our need according to His riches in glory by Christ Jesus (Phil. 4:19). He provides "all sufficiency in all things" so that we "may have an abundance for every good work" (2 Cor. 9:8). He "is able to do exceedingly abundantly above all that we ask or think, according to the power that works in us" (Eph. 3:20).

Finally, at the end of life's journey, He supplies an abundant entrance "into the everlasting kingdom of our Lord and Savior Jesus Christ" (2 Pet. 1:11).

Human language is inadequate to describe the manifold generosity of the Lord. It is too awesome to picture. But what we know of it should cause us to refrain from ever complaining and to thank Him with all our hearts. Dorothy Grimes said through her poem "God's Extravagance,"

> More sky than man can see,
> More sea than he can sail,
> More sun than he can bear to watch,
> More stars than he can scale,
> More breath than he can breathe,
> More yield than he can sow,
> More grace than he can comprehend,
> More love than he can know.

Note

1. Chocolate lovers will be interested to know that the Swedish Christian botanist who classified and gave Latin names to plants and animals, Carl von Linné (Linnaeus, 1707–78), labeled chocolate *theobroma* (Godfood).

— 25 —

Fair, Just, and Right

Righteous are You, O LORD,
And upright are Your judgments.

—Psalm 119:137

God is absolutely righteous. He always acts with fairness and equity. He invariably does what is right. In fact, an easy way to understand righteousness is to concentrate on the first five letters: *r-i-g-h-t*. That's it. God does what is right—without exception.

Daniel spoke eloquently of the righteousness of God:

> O Lord, righteousness belongs to You, but to us shame of face, as it is this day—to the men of Judah, to the inhabitants of Jerusalem and all Israel, those near and those far off in all the coun-

151

tries to which You have driven them, because of
the unfaithfulness which they have committed
against You. . . . Therefore the LORD has kept
the disaster in mind, and brought it upon us; for
the LORD our God is righteous in all the works
which He does though we have not obeyed His
voice (9:7, 14).

Here the prophet vindicated the Lord for all He
had done, even if much of it had been bitter
medicine for the people. He said, in effect,
"Lord, You are righteous, and You have acted
fairly and honorably. We have received exactly
what we deserved!"

The Lord said,

> Tell and bring forth your case;
> Yes, let them take counsel together.
> Who has declared this from ancient time?
> Who has told it from that time?
> Have not I, the LORD?
> And there is no other God besides Me,
> A just God and a Savior;
> There is none besides Me (Isa. 45:21).

Just is a synonym for *righteous*. The Lord is a
just God and a Savior. No other God can compare with Him.

Paul loved to dwell on the righteousness of
God. In Romans 3, for instance, he explains
how the gospel plan of salvation solves a divine

dilemma. It tells how a righteous God can justify ungodly sinners and still be righteous in doing so. He does not condone sin or excuse it. He pays the full penalty of sin in the substitutionary death of His beloved Son. Now God can justify all those who receive His Son as Lord and Savior. This solution to the divine dilemma is told poetically by the hymn writer Albert Midlane:

> The perfect righteousness of God
> Is witnessed in the Savior's blood;
> 'Tis in the Cross of Christ we trace
> His righteousness, yet wondrous grace.
>
> God could not pass the sinner by,
> His sin demands that he must die;
> But in the Cross of Christ we see
> How God can save us righteously.
>
> The sin is on the Savior laid,
> 'Tis in His blood sin's debt is paid;
> Stern Justice can demand no more,
> And Mercy can dispense her store.
>
> The sinner who believes is free,
> Can say, "The Savior died for me";
> Can point to the atoning blood,
> And say, "This made my peace with God."

The psalmist said, "Mercy and truth have met together; righteousness and peace have kissed" (Ps. 85:10). Whether he knew it or not, the psalmist was anticipating Calvary. There mercy could flow out freely to believing sinners because all the demands of truth had been met. There peace could be offered through faith because the sin question had been handled righteously. At the Cross, in a very special way, the attributes of God met together in loving and joyful union.

The truth of God's righteousness is designed to have a practical influence on our lives. If He is just, fair, and impartial, we must be, too, especially since we are His representatives. One of the marks of a Christian is the practice of righteousness (1 John 3:10). We must always strive to have a conscience that is void of offense toward God and others. This will mean that we will be righteous in all our dealings. We will be scrupulously honest; our word will be our bond. We will avoid anything in the way of shady deals, income tax evasion, bribery, cheating, lawbreaking, or false weights and measures. We will be impartial, causing our benefits to reach the just and the unjust. We will not judge by appearance; we will judge with righteous judgment. We do not pad the expense account, and we swear to our own hurt and do not change (Ps. 15:4). That is, we follow through with agreements, contracts, and business dealings, regardless of what it might cost us.

Then, too, we should adore God's righteousness. We should be thankful that He saves us righteously, He continues to forgive us righteously after we are saved (1 John 1:9), and He is righteous in all His dealings with us. Even if He afflicts us, He is righteous in doing it. It is an unspeakable blessing to know that our God is infinitely righteous.

God's righteousness is practically synonymous with His justice,[1] and this involves serious implications for the unsaved. When the Lord sits on the great white throne, His judgment will be absolutely righteous. His verdict will be based on the truth, the whole truth, and nothing but the truth. He will show no respect for persons. His judgments will deal with people's secrets as well as with their sins of commission and omission. His decisions will be based on perfect knowledge of everything and will be completely impartial. No sinful person should ever ask God for justice. If we received justice, we would all be doomed and damned. What we need is grace! As Count Nicolaus von Zinzendorf so aptly phrased it,

> Jesus, Thy blood and righteousness
> My beauty are, my glorious dress,
> 'Midst flaming worlds, in these arrayed,
> With joy shall I lift up my head.

Note

1. "Righteous" and "just" generally translate the same group of Hebrew words in the Old Testament and the same group of Greek words in the New.

— 26 —

Godly Jealousy

The LORD, whose name is Jealous, is a jealous God.

—Exodus 34:14

A moment's thought will remind us that, with us, jealousy can be either good or bad. When a husband discovers another man trying to steal his wife's affections, he is justifiably jealous. But when one person is envious of another person's possessions, that kind of jealousy is inexcusable.

God is jealous but always in a good sense. He desires the undivided love and loyalty of His people, and He resents any alienation of their affections. His jealousy is completely unselfish; He knows it is not for their good to be taken up with false gods.

Most of the references to the Lord's jealousy are connected with Israel's idolatry. The chosen people had forsaken the Lord God and were worshiping idols. That was spiritual harlotry. God's jealousy waxed hot.

Here are a few of the multitudes of references to the divine jealousy:

I, the LORD your God, am a jealous God (Exod. 20:5).

For the LORD your God is a consuming fire, a jealous God (Deut. 4:24).

They provoked Him to jealousy with foreign gods; with abominations they provoked Him to anger (Deut. 32:16).

> For they provoked Him to anger
>   with their high places,
> And moved Him to jealousy with
>   their carved images (Ps. 78:58).

How long, LORD?
Will You be angry forever?
Will Your jealousy burn like fire? (Ps. 79:5).

I will be jealous for My holy name (Ezek. 39:25).

God is jealous, and the LORD avenges (Nah. 1:2).

Do we provoke the Lord to jealousy? (1 Cor. 10:22).

That latter question is as apropos today as when Paul first asked it, "Do we provoke the

Lord to jealousy?" The world system is continually seeking to divert the church from its pristine love for the Savior. The lust of the eye, the lust of the flesh, and the pride of life are on the alert to seduce the believer. We may not be tempted to worship graven images, but money, power, fame, and pleasure can become idols just as truly.

A knowledge of God's intolerance for anyone or anything that would result in loss of our exclusive devotion for Him should inspire us to be faithful to Him:

> The Lord our God is a jealous God,
> He loves with jealous fire;
> Carved images and foreign gods
> Provoke His holy ire.
>
> But His is an unselfish love
> For those redeemed by blood;
> He wants first place in all our hearts
> Since this is for our good.

— 27 —

Great Is His Faithfulness

Your faithfulness reaches to the clouds.

—Psalm 36:5

Closely connected to God's immutability, a unique attribute, is His faithfulness, or His truth, which in a small way we can also cultivate. The Lord is absolutely trustworthy in all His ways, absolutely true to His Word. No promise of His can ever fail. He can neither lie nor deceive. Because of this divine perfection, the Word of God is the surest thing in the universe. If God says something, there is no risk in believing it. In fact, a person would be foolish not to believe it. Truth is what the Lord says about anything.

The Bible is full of verses telling of God's faithfulness. Here are a few:

160

Therefore know that the LORD your God, He is God, the faithful God (Deut. 7:9).

Your faithfulness endures to all generations (Ps. 119:90).

> Through the LORD'S mercies we
>   are not consumed,
> Because His compassions fail not.
> They are new every morning;
> Great is Your faithfulness (Lam. 3:22–23).

God is faithful, by whom you were called into the fellowship of His Son, Jesus Christ our Lord (1 Cor. 1:9).

God is faithful, who will not allow you to be tempted beyond what you are able (1 Cor. 10:13).

If we confess our sins, He is faithful and just to forgive us our sins (1 John 1:9).

Jesus Christ, the faithful witness (Rev. 1:5).

Think of what we owe to the faithfulness of God! It is because he is faithful that we can know that His way of salvation is the correct one. It is because He is faithful that we can have assurance of salvation through His Word. It is because He is faithful that we can know our sins are forgiven. God's faithfulness guarantees the fulfillment of all His prophecies and promises. His faithfulness accounts for our preservation day by day. We see His faithfulness to His creatures in Genesis 8:22:

> While the earth remains,
> Seedtime and harvest,
> Cold and heat,
> Winter and summer,
> And day and night
> Shall not cease.

We might well ask, "What do we not owe to the faithfulness of God?"

But this divine virtue should serve not only as a pillow but also as a prod. We should want to be like Him. We should be faithful in our dealings with one another, prompt in keeping appointments, dependable in keeping promises. We should be true to our marriage vows. Our word should be our bond. Once having made a commitment, we should stick to it, even if it means heavy loss (Ps. 15:4). We should be scrupulously honest, avoiding exaggerations and half-truths. We should be faithful at home, in the church, and at work, living in such a way that one day we will hear Him say, "Well done, good and faithful servant" (Matt. 25:21, 23). Thomas O. Chisholm praised God's faithfulness in this way:

> Great is Thy faithfulness, O God my Father,
> There is no shadow of turning with Thee;
> Thou changest not, Thy compassions, they fail not;
> As Thou hast been Thou forever wilt be.

Refrain

Great is Thy faithfulness!
Great is Thy faithfulness!
Morning by morning new mercies I see;
All I have needed Thy hand hath provided—
Great is Thy faithfulness, Lord, unto me!

Summer and winter, and springtime and harvest,
Sun, moon and stars in their courses above,
Join with all nature in manifold witness
To Thy great faithfulness, mercy and love.[1]

Note

1. Copyright © 1923. Renewal 1951 by Hope Publishing Co., Carol Stream, IL 60188. All rights reserved. Used by permission.

— 28 —
Slow to Lose Patience

The LORD is longsuffering and abundant in mercy.

—Numbers 14:18

The longsuffering of God is His willingness and ability to show restraint and self-control in dealing with human sin, provocation, and rebellion. He could judge sin instantly, and in isolated cases He has done so.[1] Generally, however, He has endured human wickedness with marvelous forbearance and patience. The fact that any of us is here to tell the story is a tribute to the longsuffering of God!

Jehovah proclaimed Himself to Moses as "the LORD, the LORD God, merciful and gracious, longsuffering, and abounding in goodness and truth" (Exod. 34:6).

Nahum spoke of Him as "slow to anger and great in power" (1:3).

Paul asks every self-righteous moralist, "Do you despise the riches of His goodness, forbearance, and longsuffering, not knowing that the goodness of God leads you to repentance?" (Rom. 2:4).

In another place, Paul speaks of the Lord as enduring "with much longsuffering the vessels of wrath prepared for destruction" (Rom. 9:22).

In answer to the question about why God doesn't deal with sinners promptly, Peter writes, "The Lord is not slack concerning His promise, as some count slackness, but is longsuffering toward us, not willing that any should perish but that all should come to repentance" (2 Pet. 3:9).

God would be justified in punishing all sin on the spot. But He does not delight in the death of the wicked. He wants people to repent and live. Therefore, He suffers long with the insolence and hostility of people. He delays the day of judgment so that men and women and boys and girls might come to the pierced feet of Christ Jesus and acknowledge Him as Lord and Savior.

Needless to say, He wants to see His longsuffering reproduced in us, His people. He wants to see us bearing up patiently and triumphantly under the aggravations of life. That means we will not be quick-tempered; we will not have a short fuse. We will not fly off the handle easily. We will not seek to retaliate. Rather, we will display a conquering patience in the face of insult and ill-treatment.

An incident in one of Corrie ten Boom's books[2] illustrates this beautifully. She and her sister, Betsy, were in a concentration camp, suffering indescribable pain and indignity. Yet Betsy would tell Corrie that when they got out, they had to do something to help those people. Corrie naturally thought she was referring to their fellow prisoners. But Betsy wasn't referring to them at all. She was referring to the guards, their persecutors!

Corrie wrote, "And I wondered, not for the first time, what sort of a person she was, this sister of mine, what kind of a road she followed, while I trudged beside her on the all too solid earth."[3] Corrie saw Betsy walking a heavenly pathway while she was living only a natural life, failing to rise above flesh and blood. The truth, of course, is that both Betsy and Corrie were walking the road of longsuffering, in spite of Corrie's disclaimer.

The history of the Christian martyrs, both in olden and in modern times, is filled with almost incredible examples of longsuffering. We marvel not only that they were able to endure extreme torture but also that they prayed for their guilty assailants.

Most of us are never called upon to endure physical pain for Jesus. Our longsuffering is limited to minor annoyances, insults, ridicule, and evil speaking. However, we should thank the Lord that we are counted worthy to suffer in any way for the sake of His name.

The hymn writer Edward Denny extols the longsuffering Savior in these words:

> Thy foes might hate, despise, revile,
> Thy friends unfaithful prove;
> Unwearied in forgiveness still,
> Thy heart could only love.

Notes

1. An Old Testament example is Uzzah (2 Sam. 6:6–9). New Testament examples are Ananias and Sapphira (Acts 5:1–11).
2. Corrie ten Boom, *The Hiding Place,* p. 161.
3. Ibid.

— 29 —

Great Is the Lord

*Behold, God is great, and we do not
know Him;*
*Nor can the number of His years be
discovered.*

—Job 36:26

*He does great things, which we cannot
comprehend.*

—Job 37:5

What is the greatest thought that can occupy
the human mind? The contemplation of God.
Human intellect can find no subject more lofty
and more worthy than this. No other theme
comes close. Thinking about God is the highest
occupation, the most sublime exercise of our
mental faculties.

How grateful we should be that God has given

us minds that are able to consider His knowledge, holiness, love, power, and wisdom. True, we see through a glass darkly. But never mind! It is still a tremendous privilege to stretch our minds to the limit in contemplating His divine attributes.

I often think of the great scientists and philosophers of the world and of the tremendous issues they have grappled with. But many of them have never wrestled with the greatest issue of all—the eternal God. It seems an enormous prostitution of the human intellect to live and die without ever thinking deeply and seriously about one's Creator and Lord.

Having spent some time in the contemplation of God, we now should realize that the subject is too big for our minds to take in fully. We are like children with their little buckets at the edge of the ocean. We can fill our buckets, but the ocean is not diminished. It should not bother us that we cannot fully understand God. If we could, we would be as great as He is. Even throughout eternity we will be ceaselessly learning the wonders of His person and work. Novatian, a third-century Christian martyr, wrote,

God is greater than mind itself. His greatness cannot be conceived. Nay, could we conceive of His greatness, He would be less than the human mind which could form the conception. He is greater than all language, and no statement can express Him. Indeed, if any statement could express Him, He would be less than human speech, which could by such statement comprehend and gather up all that He is. All our thoughts about Him will be less than He, and our loftiest utterances will be trivialities in comparison with Him.[1]

Now, by way of summarizing God's attributes, let us think about His greatness as it is unfolded in the Bible. As we read various Scriptures, we will notice that the words seem to bend under the weight of the ideas. The Spirit of God harnesses human language so that we may better understand. He assigns human form and personality to God so that we can better comprehend Him. He exhausts vocabulary to express the inexpressible.

Turn first to Job 26:14. In the preceding verses, Job has given a marvelous description of the Lord. It is one of the many breathtaking portraits of God in the Old Testament, setting forth His wisdom and power in creation. Then when Job is all through, he says,

Indeed these are the mere edges of His ways,
And how small a whisper we hear of Him!
But the thunder of His power who can understand?

In other words, God is so great that we see only the fringes of His ways and we hear only a whisper of His power. If the fringes are so mind-boggling, what must the fullness be? And if the whisper is so deafening, what must the thunder be?

Moving on to Psalm 104:32, we get another insight into God's greatness. It says, "He looks on the earth, and it trembles; He touches the hills, and they smoke." A glance from God can produce an earthquake, and His touch can cause volcanic eruptions. That's power! A mere look from the Almighty causes the foundations of the earth to shift violently, and the gentle touch of His hand causes Vesuvius to pour out tons of molten lava. If such slight impulses cause such shattering cataclysms, what would the full unleashing of God's power produce?

In Psalm 113:6, we read that God "humbles Himself to behold the things that are in the heavens and in the earth." It is a beautiful way of describing the transcendence of the Lord—the fact that He is far above and beyond the limits of our experience or our universe. If we were to stand on our tiptoes, we couldn't behold the things that are in heaven. What would be an enormous stretch for us is an enormous stoop for God. The human mind cannot imagine how exalted above all creation God is.

Psalm 147:4 says, "He counts the number of the stars; he calls them all by name." Here are two marvels—the ability to count interminably without running out of numbers and to assign a myriad of names without duplication. We do not know how many stars there are, and even if we did know, we do not have words in our vocabulary to express such quantities. British astronomer Sir James Jeans once said that it's very likely that there are as many stars in the heavens as there are grains of sand on all the seashores of the world. In the light of that, it's interesting that when God made the promise of a numberless posterity to Abraham, He spoke of stars and sand in the same breath (Gen. 22:17). In counting the stars, God shows Himself to be a God of infinite capacity. In giving each one a name, He reveals Himself as a God of infinite variety.

Surely, He is the God of the telescope. But if you look back at the preceding verse, you will find that He is the God of the microscope as well: "He heals the brokenhearted and binds up their wounds" (Ps. 147:3). The One who knows every detail of the celestial expanses is vitally interested in His sorrowful creatures. Such personal concern is awesome when you consider what a speck of cosmic dust our planet is in the universe, and how tiny we are, even in comparison to the earth. Yet the same God who counts the stars and gives a distinct name to each one also stoops low in grace to heal the brokenhearted and to bind up their wounds.

The prophet Isaiah states, "In the year that

King Uzziah died, I saw the Lord sitting on a throne, high and lifted up, and the train of His robe filled the temple" (6:1). The train of His robe filled the temple! What does that mean? The train is the part of a robe that trails behind. Only here it refers not to an actual garment but to the Lord's glory—His radiance and moral excellence. Picture for a minute a wedding in Westminster Abbey where the bridal gown is so great that its train fills the whole abbey. Then transfer the picture to the Lord and His glory. If the train of His glory fills the temple, what would the full display of that glory be like?

In Isaiah 40, we have another superlative description of the Lord. God is remonstrating with His people because they have become idolaters. That is the ultimate insult—to turn from this glorious Person we've been describing and to worship graven images representing a man, a bird, a four-footed beast, or a snake. Anyone else would have destroyed humanity long ago, but the Lord pleads with men and women in longsuffering mercy:

Who has measured the waters in the hollow of His hand,
Measured heaven with a span
And calculated the dust of the earth in a measure?
Weighed the mountains in scales
And the hills in a balance?

Who has directed the Spirit of the LORD,
Or as His counselor has taught Him?
With whom did He take counsel, and who in-
    structed Him,
And taught Him in the path of justice?
Who taught Him knowledge,
And showed Him the way of understanding?
Behold, the nations are as a drop in a bucket,
And are counted as the small dust on the scales;
Look, He lifts up the isles as a very little thing.
And Lebanon is not sufficient to burn,
Nor its beasts sufficient for a burnt offering.
All nations before Him are as nothing,
And they are counted by Him less than nothing
    and worthless (Isa. 40:12–17).

Notice what this says about the God we have
been contemplating. He is so great that He measures the waters in the palm of His hand—the
Atlantic, Pacific, Indian, Arctic, and Antarctic
Oceans, and all the seas, lakes, ponds, and
rivers. He is so great that He measures heaven
"with a span." A span is the distance between
the tip of the thumb and the tip of the little fin-
ger. God's span is able to include the arch of the
heavens. He can scoop up the dust of the earth
in the third part of a measure (about two
bushels). He can weigh the majestic mountains
and hills in His scales; to Him, they are very insignificant. The mightiest empires in the world
are equivalent to the last remaining drop in a

bucket—no more important than dust on the druggist's scales. If you were to take all the cedars of Lebanon for firewood and all its animals for sacrifice, the burnt offering would be utterly insufficient for such a great God.

Nahum wrote,

> The LORD is slow to anger and great in power,
> And will not at all acquit the wicked.
> The LORD has His way
> In the whirlwind and in the storm,
> And the clouds are the dust of His feet (1:3).

Think of that! The tornado and the storm have their way with us, but God has His way with them. To us, the clouds resemble towering Himalayas, but He is so high and great that they are no more than dust under His feet. William Cowper said it well: "He plants His footsteps in the sea and rides upon the storm." The winds and the waves obey His will.

And then in the book of Habakkuk, we have another great vision of God in His solitary, unparalleled splendor:

> God came from Teman,
> The Holy One from Mount Paran. Selah.
> His glory covered the heavens,
> And the earth was full of His praise.
> His brightness was like the light;
> He had rays flashing from His hand;
> And there His power was hidden (3:3–4).

The question that He leaves for us is, If this is His hidden power, what must its full revelation be?

It is important that we have great thoughts of God. If we reduce Him to our level, our lives will be impoverished accordingly. If our God is too small, we will never rise to greatness in His kingdom. Frederick William Faber sums it up:

> O how the thought of God attracts and draws the
> heart from earth,
> And sickens it of passing shows and dissipating
> mirth!
> 'Tis not enough to save our souls, to shun eternal
> fires;
> The thought of God will rouse the heart to more
> sublime desires.

Note

1. Novatian, *On the Trinity*, pp. 26–27.

Conclusion:

This Is Our God

Through all eternity to Thee
A joyful song I'll raise;
But, oh! eternity's too short
To utter all Thy praise!

—Joseph Addison

A book on the attributes of God can never be finished. The computer may stop and the printing press lie silent, but the surface of the subject has scarcely been scratched. It is so vast that it can never be exhausted in this life, and even eternity will not be sufficient to explore its height, depth, length, and breadth.

We can know God as He is revealed in the Bible and in the person of Christ. And yet, how little we really know of Him! We can see Him through a glass darkly, but we can never fully fathom Him. Comprehending Him completely is beyond the skill of angels or of human beings.

After we have ransacked the universe for superlatives with which to describe Him, we come back with the confession that not even a fraction has been told. All the vocabularies of all languages are feeble to tell forth His excellencies. John Darwell, the English hymn writer, was right when he said that if we "join all the glorious names of wisdom, love, and power that mortals ever knew, that angels ever bore, all are too mean[1] to speak His worth, too mean to set the Savior forth."

Just as God is infinite, so are His attributes. His holiness is absolute. His sovereignty is complete. His righteousness is perfect. He is utterly unchangeable, totally faithful, and limitless in power. His knowledge is inexhaustible, and His presence is boundless. He is wise beyond measure, loving beyond description, and gracious beyond imagination. If His mercy is high beyond calculation, His wrath is deep beyond measure. His goodness is an ocean without shores, and His longsuffering is a sky without horizons.

God's existence is without beginning or end. He owes it to no one and nothing outside Himself, and He does not depend on anyone or anything outside Himself for His well-being or happiness. He is utterly incomprehensible and supremely transcendent. And what more can we say? He is greater than the total of all His attributes.

All the attributes of God are in perfect balance. None is exercised at the expense of another, and none is greater than another. We may be loving but not altogether righteous. We may have great knowledge but not great wisdom. But all God's characteristics are perfect, and they coexist in perfect harmony.

A God so great is greatly to be praised! He is

greatly to be feared in the assembly of the saints,
And to be held in reverence by all those around
　　Him (Ps. 89:7).

For this is God,
Our God forever and ever;
He will be our guide
Even to death (Ps. 48:14).

The words of Ernst Lange summarize so much about our God:

O God, Thou bottomless abyss!
Thee to perfection who can know?
O height immense! What words suffice?
Thy countless attributes to show?

Unfathomable depths Thou art;
Oh plunge me in Thy mercy's sea!
Void of true wisdom is my heart;
With love embrace and cover me.

Eternity Thy fountain was,
Which, like Thee, no beginning knew:
Thou wast ere time began his race,
Ere glowed with stars the ethereal blue.

Unchangeable, all-perfect Lord,
Essential life's unbounded sea,
What lives and moves, lives by Thy word;
It lives, and moves, and is from Thee.

Greatness unspeakable is Thine,
Greatness, whose undiminished ray,
When short-lived worlds are lost, shall shine;
When earth and heaven are fled away.

Note

1. Darwell was using the word *mean* in the sense of "inferior," "shabby," and "of little value."

Bibliography

Books

Baxter, J. Sidlow. *The Master Theme of the Bible: Grateful Studies in the Comprehensive Saviorhood of Our Lord Jesus Christ.* Wheaton: Tyndale, 1973.

Blanchard, John, compiler. *Gathered Gold: A Treasury of Quotations for Christians.* Welwyn, England: Evangelical Press, 1984.

Brand, Dr. Paul, and Philip Yancey. *Fearfully and Wonderfully Made.* Grand Rapids: Zondervan, 1980.

Chafer, Lewis Sperry. *Systematic Theology.* Vol. 1. Dallas: Dallas Seminary Press, 1953.

Charnock, Stephen. *The Existence and Attributes of God.* 1969. Reprint. Minneapolis: Klock and Klock, 1977.

Cutting, George. *Light for Anxious Souls.* Oak Park, Ill.: Bible Truth Publishers, 1975.

Elliot, Elisabeth. *Shadow of the Almighty.* New York: Harper and Bros., 1958.

———. *A Slow and Certain Light.* Waco: Word, 1976.

Erdman, Charles R. *The Epistle of Paul to the Romans.* Philadelphia: Westminster Press, 1919.

Evans, William. *The Great Doctrines of the Bible.* Chicago: Moody, 1939.

Hunt, Dave. *Global Peace.* Eugene, Oreg.: Harvest House, 1990.

Hymns of Truth and Praise. Belle Chasse, La.: Truth and Praise, 1971.

181

Julian of Norwich. *Revelations of Divine Love.* London: Methuen & Co., 1920.

Novatian. *On the Trinity.* New York: Macmillan, 1919.

Packer, J. I. *Knowing God.* London: Hodder and Stoughton, 1973.

Pierson, Arthur T. "The Gift of Righteousness." In *The Ministry of Keswick.* 1st series. Grand Rapids: Zondervan, 1963.

Pink, A. W. *The Attributes of God.* Swengel, Pa.: Reiner Publications, n.d.

Spurgeon, Charles Haddon. *Treasury of the Bible.* Grand Rapids: Baker Book House, 1981.

————— . *Treasury of David.* Vols. 4 and 5. Grand Rapids: Baker Book House, 1981.

ten Boom, Corrie. *The Hiding Place.* Washington Depot, Conn.: Chosen Books, 1971.

Thomas, I. D. E., compiler. *The Golden Treasury of Puritan Quotations.* Chicago: Moody Press, 1975.

Thompson, Francis. *Poetical Works.* London: University Press, 1913.

Tozer, A. W. *The Knowledge of the Holy.* Reprint. Bromley, Kent, England: STL Books, 1981.

Periodical Articles

Davis, Malcolm. "The Transcendence of God." *Precious Seed Magazine,* May–June 1984.

Horlock, M. "The Eternal God." *Precious Seed Magazine,* Sept.–Oct. 1987.

Ponte, Lowell. "How Color Affects Your Moods." *Reader's Digest,* July 1982.

Daily Notes of the Scripture Union (Foreman).